Gilles & Jeanne

MICHEL TOURNIER

Gilles & Jeanne

*Translated from the French
by Alan Sheridan*

GROVE WEIDENFELD
New York

Published by Grove Weidenfeld
A division of Wheatland Corporation
841 Broadway
New York, NY 10003-4793

First published in France in 1983 by Editions Gallimard
First published in English in Great Britain in 1987 by Methuen London

Library of Congress Cataloging-in-Publication Data

Tournier, Michel.
  [Gilles & Jeanne. English]
  Gilles & Jeanne/Michel Tournier; translated from the French by
Alan Sheridan.—1st Grove Weidenfeld ed.
      p.   cm.
  ISBN 0-8021-0021-X (alk. paper)
  1. Rais, Gilles de, 1404–1440—Fiction. 2. Joan, of Arc, Saint,
1412–1431—Fiction. 3. France—History—Charles VII, 1422–1461
—Fiction.   I. Sheridan, Alan. II. Title. III. Title: Gilles and
Jeanne.
PQ2680.083G513   1990
843'.914—dc20   89-71436
                                                            CIP

Manufactured in the United States of America

Printed on acid-free paper

First American Edition 1990

10 9 8 7 6 5 4 3 2 1

It was at the end of the winter of 1429 – on 25 February – at the Château de Chinon that their destinies crossed. Gilles de Rais was one of those country squires from Brittany and the Vendée who had thrown in their lot with the Dauphin Charles in his struggle against the English army. In the name of Henri VI, King of England – who was still only a child – his uncle John, Duke of Bedford, ruled as regent. But he also ruled in Paris, had occupied Normandy and was laying siege to Orléans, the gateway to the south of France.

At Chinon there was much talk, but little action. Did those politicians and soldiers, who had had their fill of failures and defeats, still believe in the cause they were defending? Only the Dauphin Charles dared to declare with confidence that he was the son of Charles VI, despite all the infidelities of his mother, Isabeau of Bavaria. A brilliant but heartless society chattered and gossiped under the panelled ceiling of the throne room, lit by the blaze from the huge fireplace.

The court was expecting a strange visit – one that promised to provide them with some entertainment. A sixteen-year-old peasant girl was on her way from the borderlands of Lorraine, declaring that she had been sent by the King of Heaven to save the kingdom of France. The Dauphin had decided to see her. For the courtiers this visit provided a welcome break: such entertainments were few and far between in that gloomy season of exile. But Charles, fearful, harried by ominous news, surrounded by gloomy prognostications, probably harboured some feeble, secret hope, as a sick man abandoned by his doctors might turn to a quack.

At that late hour, the throne room was crowded. Over five hundred knights, lit by a forest of flaming torches, suddenly stood stock-still, their eyes fixed on the door. There appeared, with firm step, what looked like a young page boy, whose clothes of black and grey coarse cloth formed a striking contrast with their brocades, their furs of vair and ermine, and their tunics of embroidered silk. Bright green eyes, a bony face with high cheekbones, a helmet of close-cut dark hair and that subtle, almost natural animal gait acquired by those who are in the habit of walking barefoot . . . Truly this creature came from elsewhere and stood out in the midst of the courtiers, like a young fawn among the turkeys, peacocks and guinea fowl of a farmyard.

She had sent the Dauphin a peremptory message:

'I have travelled fifty leagues through armed bands to bring you help. I have many good things to tell you. I shall be able to recognize you among all the people present.'

The gentlemen had laughed. Charles had smiled, in his usual forced way. Between the boy-girl who claimed to be sent from God and the false King, son of a crazed cuckold and a whore-like Queen, a strange game of concealment and recognition was to take place.

'She claims to be able to recognize me among everybody,' Charles had said. 'Well, let her, then! Let us put her to the test. Let her come in and recognize the Dauphin among everybody!'

Thereupon he rose from the throne, which he yielded to the Comte de Clermont – the very same who had been held in captivity by John the Fearless and freed on condition that he marry his daughter Agnès.

So there he stood, the young page with the bright eyes.

He looked around for the Dauphin. He hesitated in front of Clermont, then, seeing Charles, went up to him and knelt before him. How had he recognized him? By his heavy nose, his drooping mouth, his shaven head, his bandy legs? But *he* did not recognize *her*. He saw only a boy who wanted to pass himself off as a maid, a crank who claimed to be in daily commerce with the saints in heaven.

Yet the young page was already communicating some of his strength of conviction to that shadow of a king. With a few words, he swept away the doubts that hung over him like a flight of vultures. *'I tell you from God that you are the true heir of France and a king's son, and I am sent to take you to Rheims that you may be crowned and consecrated.'* So much enthusiasm must have some effect. A blush came to Charles's cheeks and his eyes lit up. In Jeanne, he had recognized himself, a king from and by God. But he was far from recognizing her.

'Jeanne of Domrémy, you claim to be a girl sent by God,' he said. 'Are you willing to submit to the tests that I shall impose on you?'

'Lord Dauphin, you command, Jeanne obeys,' she replied.

And he explained to her that she looked so much like a boy that he wanted her to be examined by two matrons present there: Jeanne de Preuilly, Dame de Gaucourt, and Jeanne de Mortemer, Dame de Trèves.

Poor Jeanne! It was the first time she had been undressed. It would not be the last. Meanwhile, the two matrons swelled with pride, in all their ridiculous finery. They rubbed their heavy, beringed hands together before feeling the virgin's belly and the horseman's thighs of the young page.

The other test was to answer questions on religious

matters put by churchmen, learned clerks and theologians, who were to meet for this purpose in the good city of Poitiers.

Thus Jeanne had recognized Charles, who recognized himself through her. But in order to recognize Jeanne in turn, he required the opinion of experts as to her sex and opinions. Yet there was one man who recognized Jeanne at first glance, as soon as she entered the throne room. This was Gilles. Yes, he immediately recognized in her everything he loved, everything he had waited for for so long: a boy, a companion in arms and play, and at the same time a woman, a saint haloed with light. It was indeed a prodigious miracle that such rare and incompatible qualities should be found together in the same person. And the miracle continued when he heard the Dauphin end the audience with these words: 'For the time being, Jeanne, I place you in the charge of my cousin, the Duke of Alençon, and my liegeman the Sire de Rais, who will take good care of you.'

From then on, the Dauphin accommodated Jeanne in a wing of the Château de Couldray, with women and a page, Louis de Coutes, who was scarcely younger than she since she was then only fourteen, to serve her.

In the morning, she attended mass with the Dauphin. The rest of the time she tried her strength and skill with her companions Jean and Gilles, and it was very rare for her not to be victorious with racket, sword, spear or bow.

One day, Alençon said to Rais as he watched her perform acrobatics on a horse at the gallop: 'I'm not surprised she's a virgin. Unless he liked boys, no man would take it into his head to approach her.'

These words seemed to hurt Rais, who responded vehemently: 'And what about me? You astonish me, cousin. When one likes boys, one considers that there is nothing like a boy, a real boy, for love. But, in fact, there is something else in Jeanne that explains why she is a virgin.'

'Something else?'

'Can't you see the purity that radiates from her face? From her whole body? There is an obvious innocence throughout her body that absolutely discourages licentious words and over-familiar gestures. Yes, a childish innocence, with something more – how can I describe it? – a light that is not of this world.'

'A light from heaven?' Alençon asked, raising his eyebrows.

'From heaven, exactly. If Jeanne is neither a girl nor a boy, then she must be an angel.'

They fell silent and looked at Jeanne, who was smiling as she stood, arms outstretched to form a cross, on the rump of her galloping horse. And, indeed, she did seem to glide along on invisible wings above the animal as it furiously pounded the earth with its iron shoes.

A lot of nonsense has been talked about Gilles's early years, thus committing the common error of projecting the future on to the past. Knowing how he ended up, people are determined to make him a vicious child, a perverse youth, a cruel young man. They have been pleased to imagine all the premonitory signs of the crimes of his maturity. In the absence of any documentation, it is permissible to take the opposite line to this tradition of the 'monster-coming-to-birth'. So we shall take it that Gilles de Rais, before that fateful meeting at Chinon, had been a fairly typical lad of his time, no better, but no worse than any other, of average intelligence, but deeply religious – at a time when it was common to have everyday commerce with God, Jesus, the Virgin and the saints – and doomed, in short, to the fate of a country squire from a particularly backward

11

province.

He was born in November 1404 in the Black Tower of the fortress of Champtocé, on the banks of the Loire. The master of the house, his maternal grandfather Jean de Craon, governed his estates with a harshness and unscrupulousness that were a source of wonder even in those violent times. Gilles was eleven when, in the same year, he lost both his father and his mother. Craon tore up his son-in-law's will and took over both the guardianship of young Gilles and the management of his fortune. His obsession was to marry the child into one of the biggest fortunes in the region. Thus, at thirteen, Gilles was engaged to Jeanne Peynel, a four-year-old orphan, who was also one of the richest heiresses in Normandy. To achieve this, Craon had to pay off her guardian's debts. But the Paris Parlement opposed the engagement: they would have to wait until the girl came of age. Two years later, he engineered an even more lucrative union – this time with the niece of Jean V, Duke of Brittany – but this, too, failed to transpire. Gilles was sixteen by the time his grandfather succeeded in his plans. The prey was called Catherine de Thouars, and her property in Poitou was most conveniently situated next to the barony of Rais. There was little hope that the father would accept this union – which, in any case, was incestuous, for the couple were cousins: but at the time he was waging war in Champagne. In late November 1420, Craon organized the forced seizure of the fiancée by her claimant. Gilles greatly enjoyed this expedition, which was more ridiculous than dangerous, and its romantic consequences: a secret marriage, outside the respective parishes of the spouses; vain threats from the Bishop of Angers; intervention in the Court of Rome; fines; pardon; solemn nuptial blessing in the church of Saint-Maurille-de-Chalonnes.

But Gilles soon realized that he could expect nothing from this fat, lazy girl, who was quite hopeless at hunting and tourneys, who was afraid of weapons, of horses, of game, of everything, it seemed. It took him nine years to give her a child – and to forget her in the Château de Pouzauges. At Chinon, he found in Jeanne the exact opposite of Catherine. He found in the Maid the intoxicating, dangerous fusion of sanctity and war.

For Jeanne's unexpected arrival at the Dauphin's court meant the resumption of the war.

At Poitiers, she had replied with a pure heart to the theologians' questions. *In the end the clerks concluded that there was in her nothing evil, nothing contrary to the Catholic faith, and, given the plight in which the King and kingdom found themselves, since the King and those inhabitants who were faithful to him were on the verge of despair and could expect help of no kind if it did not come from God, the King might well make use of her.* Thus wrote Jean Barbin, barrister at the Parlement.

So she was given *carte blanche*. Her first action was

to send a message to the English to the effect that they should go back across the Channel and return from whence they came, or they would regret it. It was the first time that she had made direct contact with them. Thus the vague rumours that there was a witch who had brought the pseudo-King of Bourges under her spell were confirmed. Damn the witch!

Everybody went off to Tours, where the army raised by the Dauphin assembled. A suit of white armour was made for Jeanne, together with a standard on which was painted a picture of the Saviour seated among the clouds of heaven, blessing a fleur-de-lys held out to him by an angel. Her voices had told her that she was to wear an ancient sword, buried unknown to all behind the altar of the church of Sainte-Catherine-de-Fierbois. A man was sent off to Fierbois. He rummaged around and exhumed the sword – it was rusty, but in excellent condition.

In all this business, in which were mingled politics, the preparations for a military campaign and Christian magic, Gilles served as an expert and diligent liegeman. He was a man and he was a professional. He followed Jeanne, as the body obeys the soul, as she herself obeyed her 'voices'. On certain evenings, when the curfew had silenced the camp and they found themselves alone together, they talked. Gilles – like Jeanne, like most men and women of that time – lived on the confines of the natural and the supernatural. But his experience and personal inclination had shown him more devils and evil

14

spirits than saints and guardian angels.

'Like you, I believe that we live surrounded by angels and saints,' he said to her one night. 'I also believe that there is never a shortage of devils and evil fairies trying to make us stumble on to the road to wickedness. But I've heard you say, Jeanne, that they speak to you and that all you have done was inspired by the supernatural voices you heard.'

'As far as devils and evil fairies are concerned,' she replied, 'I have met none to this day. But who knows what the future may bring!'

Brought up in the damp gloom of a fortress, Gilles found it difficult to imagine her peasant childhood, exposed to all weathers.

'But in the copses and root-entangled caves that lie deep in the hillsides,' he went on, 'you know, you who have tended animals, you must know that there are dwarfs and lemures who cast spells on people.'

Jeanne did remember.

'Quite close to the town of Domrémy where I was born, there is a tree known as the Ladies' Tree. It's a great beech tree, centuries old. In the spring it is as beautiful as a lily and its branches reach down to the ground. Some people call it the Fairies' Tree. In the shade of its branches is a spring. Those who are sick with fever drink the water of that spring and are cured. In the month of Mary, the girls and boys of Domrémy decorate the branches of the Ladies' Tree with garlands. They lay a cloth beside the spring and eat together. Then they play and dance. I did that

15

with my friends, but I never saw or heard tell of dwarfs or any other creature of the Devil.'

Gilles was dazzled by such sweet innocence, but he remained unconvinced.

'And yet the Devil and his court exist. I sometimes feel them brush past me and they whisper obscure things in my ears that I can't understand and that I am afraid I *will* understand one day. You, too, hear voices.'

'Yes, I was thirteen the first time. A voice came to me about noon, in summer, in my father's garden. I heard a voice that came from the direction of the church. I was very afraid at first. But then I realized that it was an angel's voice, St Michael's to be precise. He told me that St Catherine and St Margaret would come and see me and that I was to do as they told me and that I was to believe that their orders came from God.'

'What did those voices tell you to do?'

'Above all, they told me to be a good child and that God would help me. Then they told me of the pitiful state in which the kingdom of France found itself and that I ought to go and help my King.'

'Did you say anything to your parish priest about these visions?'

'No, only to Robert de Baudricourt, captain of the city of Vaucouleurs, and also to my King. My voices didn't tell me to keep what they said to myself, but I was very afraid to reveal my plan for fear of the Burgundians, and also lest my father prevent me
16

making my journey.'

'How did you leave Domrémy without arousing suspicion?'

'I went to my uncle's. He is Durand Laxart, a notable of Durey-le-Petit, a short distance from Vaucouleurs. I told him that I wanted to go to France to see the Dauphin and to have him crowned, since it was written that France would be lost by a woman[1] and saved by a virgin. It was Durand who took me to the Sire de Baudricourt.'

'And what did Captain Baudricourt say to your Uncle Durand?'

'That Robert told my uncle to give me a good thrashing and take me back home.'

'Which is what he did.'

'Which is what he did. But six months later I was back again, and this time I managed to convince Baudricourt. And the people of Vaucouleurs gave me boy's clothes, which I have not given up since. And they bought me a horse for twelve francs.'

'And what about your voices?'

'They did not leave me in peace, but were constantly encouraging and exhorting me.'

Gilles, who, because of his immense fortune, knew only violence and machinations to achieve often pitiful ends, was astonished at the spectacle of so much weakness and simplicity overcoming all resistance and scepticism in the name of some grandiose purpose.

'So the Fairies' Tree said nothing,' he concluded,

'and you were advised by voices coming from the direction of the church. Jeanne, I believe each of us has his voices. Good voices and bad voices. I am the little bull of Champtocé, born in the Black Tower of the fortress. I was brought up by my grandfather, Jean de Craon, a great lord, but also a great scoundrel. The voices I heard in my childhood and youth were always those of evil and sin. Jeanne, you have come not only to save the Dauphin Charles and his kingdom. You must also save the young lord Gilles de Rais! Make him hear your voice. Jeanne, I never want to leave your side. Jeanne, you are a saint, make a saint of me!'

And war broke out again.

On Friday 29 April 1429, Gilles and Jeanne entered Orléans, welcomed by a delirious crowd 'carrying a large number of torches and expressing such joy, as if they had seen God himself descend among them,' one witness wrote.

On Wednesday 11 May, they went to Loches in order to inform the Dauphin officially of the liberation of Orléans and to persuade him to go to Rheims to be anointed King. On Saturday 18 June, the English were defeated at Patay, and their leader, John Talbot, was taken prisoner. Auxerre, Troyes and Châlons rallied to the Dauphin and sent him contingents to honour his coronation.

The cathedral of Notre-Dame-de-Reims is the cradle of the French monarchy. The Holy Ampulla containing an inexhaustible oil is preserved in the church of Saint-Remy. Indeed, in 496, Remy received it from a bird that flew down from heaven to anoint Clovis, the first Christian king. Gilles de Rais was given the honour of going to fetch it, in accordance with a ritual a thousand years old[2]. The ceremony took place on 17 July 1429. With Jeanne on his right and Gilles on his left, the future King knelt on the altar steps. He should have been surrounded by the twelve peers of the kingdom, but there were absences and betrayals. In particular, the Duke of Alençon replaced the Duke of Burgundy, who had sided with the English. The archbishop officiated. The Sire d'Albret held the sword. The Maid held the banner aloft. Alençon dubbed the Dauphin knight. The archbishop anointed and crowned the new king. Then Jeanne threw herself at his feet, kissed his knees, and said, weeping, 'Gentle King, thus the will of God is done, by which you were to go to Rheims to receive the crown, so that all should know that you alone are the true King.'

But, after this apotheosis, there was to be nothing but decline, defeat and horror. Charles fell back into his usual apathy, despite the fervent welcome given him by the good people wherever he went and the exhortations of Jeanne, who persuaded him to march on Paris. The summer went by, with endless delays and diplomatic negotiations. It was not until September that they finally attacked the kingdom's capital. Finally, on 7 September, twelve thousand men of Armagnac, commanded by Gilles and Jeanne, with carts and carriages filled with logs and faggots to fill the moats, attacked the Portes Saint-Honoré and Saint-Denis. Jeanne called upon the besieged citizens to surrender.

'Surrender to us quickly, for Jesus's sake, and make your submission to King Charles!'

From the top of the ramparts they responded with a volley of oaths and a shower of missiles.

'Whore of a cowgirl! If the Armagnacs were men, you'd talk less of your maidenhead!'

They crossed the first moat, which was dry. The second was enormous: fifty feet across filled with the high waters of the Seine. Jeanne was the first to reach its edge. She moved forward into the water, sounding the bottom with the staff of her standard to find the best place to cross. They would turn over the carriages if necessary. The pontoon-builders went about their business under a hail of arrows and tiles. Suddenly Jeanne's standard-bearer had his foot pierced by an arrow from a cross-bow. He raised the visor of his helmet to examine his wound. He then received a second arrow on the forehead and fell forward. Dead. Jeanne picked up his standard, but she had also been touched above the knee. The Sire de Gaucourt led her away, despite her furious protestations.

'We should have gone on and crossed the moats! Paris was ours!'

Gaucourt pointed out to her that Alençon and

Clermont had been forced out of the pig market, from which they had dominated the situation. She herself had to have her wound dressed. The sun was going down. Tomorrow the fight would begin again.

'Tomorrow, always tomorrow! I have been waiting for months for tomorrow. But I know that I must act quickly. My days are numbered. I shall last a year, hardly more.'

Lying on a camp bed in her tent, she paid no attention to her wounded leg, to the ugly wound from which the blood trickled over her knee. She was still complaining bitterly about the lost day.

'Retreat when all was to be won! The city was taken.'

Apothecaries and surgeons invaded the tent to treat her. She brushed them aside angrily.

'Go! Get out all of you! I don't need unguents, marmot grease or theriaca to be cured. God and his saints will see to my wound.'

The doctors poured out of the tent. One man however remained, sitting on a tall drum. It was Gilles. He said nothing for a long time, then, in the end, he spoke.

'You are still in the fever of combat,' he said. 'You can't feel your wound. In an hour you'll have recovered your sang-froid. Then it will begin to hurt. It will hurt all night.'

'It will hurt if God so wills. There is no joy or pain that does not come from God. What are you doing here?'

Gilles looked at her, smiling vaguely.

'Looking at you, warming my heart in your presence.'

'Do you take me for a brazier?'

'There is a fire inside you. I believe it to be from God, but it may be from hell. Good and evil are always so close to one another. Of all creatures, Lucifer was the most like God.'

'You're a good theologian for a soldier. Your companions maintain that you've no more brains than a two-year-old bull.'

'True. I have never had more than one idea in my head. I am neither a scholar nor a philosopher. I can hardly read and write. But since you came to Chinon, on 25 February, this year, that one thought that my poor head is capable of containing is called Jeanne.'

Jeanne looked at him suspiciously.

'Don't try to court me, young bull. Jeanne is not one of those girls to be pulled down into a ditch by a soldier!'

Gilles got up and came and knelt before her.

'Fear nothing, Jeanne, I love you for what you are. The Maid of Orléans. The boy-girl who saved France and anointed the King. The gentle companion in arms who charged the enemy with me boot to boot at Patay. Heavens, how we laid into them, the goddams, eh!'

Jeanne couldn't help smiling when she remembered.

'But I love you above all for the purity that is

inside you and that nothing can tarnish.'

Looking down, he saw her wound.

'Will you accept the only kiss that I ask of you?'

He bent down and laid his lips for a long time on Jeanne's wound.

He then stood up and licked his lips.

'I have communicated with your blood. I am bound to you forever. Henceforth I shall follow you wherever you go. Whether to heaven or to hell!'

Jeanne bestirred herself and stood up.

'Before going to heaven or to hell, I want to go to Paris!'

As if to answer her, an officer burst into the tent.

'By order of the King, I have to inform you that the retreat has been sounded. The King's retinue has left the heights of Montmartre for Saint-Denis. Tomorrow it will fall back to the banks of the Loire.'

Jeanne could not believe what she had heard.

'At first light, we can attempt an assault downstream of the Ile Saint-Denis by the pontoon bridge. Montmorency has spies in the fortress. We shall offer the King of France his capital on a plate!'

But these were dreams. The officer had to admit to Jeanne that in two hours the pontoon bridge would not be there. It was being dismantled on the King's orders.

Jeanne was dumbstruck. Yet, for six months, she had known her sovereign, with his shilly-shallying, his retreats from undertakings, his minor betrayals, which as they accumulated looked like betrayal pure and simple.

'My God,' she sighed, 'why is Charles so obstinately determined to get back to his little bedroom!'

Gilles had hardly heard the disastrous news. What mattered to him was neither Paris, nor the glory of the King of France.

'I shall follow you everywhere,' he repeated, 'to heaven and to hell!'

Autumn passed and it was winter. Jeanne, who knew that she had only a year before her – hardly more – was cooling her heels in that dreamy, frivolous court. Alençon had been taken from her and sent to Normandy. Gilles had mysteriously disappeared. Jeanne followed the court, from one castle to another, to Bourges, Sully, Montfaucon-en-Berry. To satisfy in part her thirst for action, she laid siege to Saint-Pierre-le-Moutiers – successfully – then to La Charité-sur-Loire – unsuccessfully. The King tried to coax her out of her ill temper. He dowered her, ennobled her, exempted the inhabitants of Greux and Domrémy from taxes. Then the dramatic events at Compiègne occurred.

She went to that city on 23 May 1430 with between three to four hundred men in order to confront the Duke of Burgundy, who was preparing to attack it.

On the morning of the twenty-fourth, she was told that a large-scale skirmish was taking place in front of the city. Jeanne threw herself into the mêlée and gave chase to a detachment of fleeing Burgundians. She did not listen to those who begged her not to risk going further into enemy terrain. When at last she decided to turn back, it was too late. Her retreat was cut off. She fought bitterly to carve out a passage to the drawbridge. The fortress commander, Guillaume de Flavy, seeing how many Burgundians and English were approaching, ordered the drawbridge to be raised and the gates shut. An archer seized Jeanne by her cloth-of-gold cape and pulled her off her horse. The great adventure was over. It had lasted less than eighteen months. There now began a passion of tears, mud and blood that was to end on Wednesday 30 May 1431 at the stake in Rouen.

Gilles, however, retired to his estates in the Vendée. He didn't care a fig for the marshal's baton that the King had given him in recognition of his services. Neither war nor politics held his interest. All that mattered to him now was that personal, mystical adventure that had begun on the day that he had met Jeanne. But since the failure of the assault on Paris, the state of grace in which Jeanne had lived and which she had got him to share seemed to have come to an end. This was a tribulation indeed, for his life was bound up with hers and he would follow her to hell if necessary. Meanwhile, he soothed his sorrows by doing what the King – and most of the lords of that time – did: he travelled in great state from one fortress or residence to another. The astounded peasants and woodcutters stood and watched this sumptuous procession of officers and prelates followed by an impressive train of carts. No, it was not a military expedition. It was simply the Seigneur de Rais, his retinue and household on the road from Champtocé to Machecoul or from Tiffauges to Pouzauges. So vast were the Seigneur de Rais's possessions and so numerous his residences that he could certainly continue such journeys for a very long time before coming back to the same place.

But one day these movements came to a stop. News came by word of mouth, from Compiègne to the Vendée, leaving a single image imprinted on Gilles's feverish brain: Jeanne pulled from her horse by an archer clinging to her silk cape, trodden underfoot by the Burgundian rabble.

Gilles could no longer remain idle. Where was the court of France at that time? At Sully-sur-Loire, whose castle belonged to Georges de La Trémouille, who was in great favour with Charles, but had always resented Jeanne's success. Gilles hastened there and first asked for an audience with Yolande of Aragon, the King's mother-in-law. She was an imposing lady. She treated with playful familiarity this marshal of France who allowed himself the luxury of preferring the loneliness of his moors to court intrigue.

'Seigneur de Rais!' she simpered. 'What a surprise!

It's a year now since you disappeared. We were talking about you only yesterday evening. We imagined you lying low in one of your forests, like a wild boar. What have you been doing all this time? What has brought you out of your hole?'

'Madame, what has brought me out of my hole,' Gilles replied, 'is the sad news that has reached me concerning Jeanne.'

Now we are getting to it, thought Yolande. Still sticking together, those two ruffians!

'Poor little Jeanne!' she cried.

'She will not be given a fair trial at Rouen. The whole thing will be rigged to bring about her downfall.'

'What a dreadful mistake that expedition to Compiègne was!' the King's mother-in-law lamented. 'But you know, Jeanne undertook it without orders from Charles, with men that she had recruited herself. Charles didn't want to leave her in command any more. You understand, Marshal de Rais, a shepherdess obeying heavenly voices!'

'Nevertheless it was by answering those voices that she delivered Orléans and had Charles crowned at Rheims,' Gilles reminded the old lady, somewhat tactlessly.

'No doubt, no doubt, but you can't base a policy on miracles. Jeanne failed to take Paris. Because she was listening to her voices, she would take neither advice nor orders. You will recall, she said that the work would have to be carried out swiftly because she would not last beyond a year. Well, the year is up!'

'Madame, when Charles was crowned at Rheims, Jeanne stood on his right hand. I was on his left. Now Jeanne is a prisoner of the English, who want to kill her. I have come to ask the King what he intends to do to save her.'

Yolande was very vexed. Warlords could certainly be a nuisance in peacetime! This young man would have done better to stay in his forests.

'Charles is very busy,' she muttered. 'I think you'll be disappointed . . .'

'I have money, men, horses,' he went on, quite undeterred. 'Above all I am determined to save Jeanne.'

Yolande gave a sigh of boredom.

'Jeanne has condemned herself. You'll have your work cut out!'

The next scene shows him with the King. He has found a legal argument which he appears to regard as unanswerable.

'Sire, Jeanne is being tried by Pierre Cauchon, Bishop of Beauvais. Now the Bishop of Beauvais comes under the jurisdiction of the Archbishop of Rheims, Monseigneur Regnault, your counsellor. Monseigneur Regnault, by virtue of his privilege, must demand that his subordinate Cauchon provide him with the documentary evidence.'

Charles, who was looking out of the window while stroking a white greyhound bitch, made an evasive gesture.

A desperate Gilles descended the castle staircase. He found himself back in the courtyard. His horse was fetched. He was about to mount it when an old soldier, who looked as lonely as Gilles, appeared on the scene. Gilles looked at him. His face lit up. It was La Hire, his old comrade-in-arms. They embraced one another.

'Where is the marshal going?' La Hire asked.

'The marshal is going home,' Gilles replied. 'There is nobody here, you hear, nobody!'

'Nobody?'

'Nobody to help me save Jeanne from the English. I have pleaded her cause with the Queen Mother and with the King himself: their ears are stopped up, their eyes shifty, their mouths lying. Nobody!'

'Nobody? And what about me, then?'

'You?'

'I, *mon maréchal*! Let's go together. Jeanne won't be surprised to see her companion Gilles and her old friend La Hire turn up. Ah! There you are! she'll say. I was expecting you. I daresay you had a good time on the way!'

Gilles took his companion off to an inn table.

'No, we are not going to have a good time on the way,' he said. 'The goddams hold the whole of Normandy. We can't attack them head on. We'll have to use cunning – slip in behind their lines with a handful of our best men.'

La Hire suggested two companies of veterans. In

December 1429, he had himself recaptured Louviers from the English. It stayed French – and he was well known and well liked there. That would be their starting point for a raid on Rouen.

The spring of 1431 was one of the coldest and wettest ever recorded by the chroniclers. The small troop, led by Rais and La Hire, wound its way through a countryside devastated by war and foreign occupation. They passed dilapidated houses and corpses of horses; crows wheeled overhead. Sometimes they had to hide when a detachment of English passed. When the number of the enemy was not too great they attacked them, but then there were losses and these were irreparable. In spite of a few lucky encounters, Gilles de Rais's men were decimated. The defences of Rouen proved formidable. They had to disperse and act under various disguises. Gilles managed to get into the city with one companion. He had no time to waste: there was a rumour that Jeanne had been condemned to the stake and was to be burnt that very week. Wounded, his clothes in rags, Gilles hardly looked better than a vagabond. Lost in the crowd, his heart heavy with hatred and grief, he watched the preparations for the execution. At the top of the pole stuck on to the pyre he could make out a scroll listing the sixteen charges of which Jeanne had been found guilty: *Jeanne, who called herself the Maid, a liar, a pernicious woman, a betrayer of the people, a soothsayer, superstitious blasphemer of God, presumptuous, unbeliever in the faith, boastful, idolatrous, cruel, dissolute, invoker of devils, apostate, schismatic, heretic.* A cardboard mitre had been stuck on her head derisively and it had fallen over her face. The stake was too high for the executioner to strangle her, as was the custom out of Christian charity, when the smoke first rose from the flames. So Jeanne had to endure inhuman torments to the end. As soon as the first flames reached her, she cried out *'Jesus! Jesus! Jesus!'* And this cry did not cease until the last gasp, throughout the entire agony. In the end, the bailiff ordered the executioner to cut down the body, so that nobody could be in any doubt. She hung there on the pole, in the swirling smoke, a poor, half-charred carcass, a bald head, one eye burst open, hanging on a swollen torso, while a terrible smell of burning flesh floated over the town.

Gilles fled the scene. A wild flight indeed. He ran through the narrow streets, climbed over walls, jumped over ditches and stumbled across fields. He fell, got to his feet again, tore his face on brambles,

34

waded through puddles, ran again, with the diabolical litany of the charges laid against Jeanne and her pitiful cries of *'Jesus! Jesus! Jesus!'* echoing endlessly in his head.

He fell, his face buried in the dark earth. He lay there, as if dead, until the first light of dawn. Then he rose to his feet. But if anyone had seen his face he would have realized that something had changed inside him: he had the face of a lying, pernicious, dissolute, blaspheming invoker of devils. But this was nothing. A beaten, broken man, he went on and buried himself in his fortresses in the Vendée. For three years he became a cocooned caterpillar. When the malign metamorphosis was complete, he emerged, an infernal angel, unfurling his wings.

The death of Jean de Craon, Gilles's grandfather and guardian, which occurred at Champtocé on 15 November 1432, put him at the head of a huge fortune and gave him free rein. Relations between the old man and the boy had been complex, for although the old villain had long chosen to see his heir as a somewhat timid disciple, he gradually discovered what a pale figure he himself cut in comparison to the abysses in which the young man's soul usually wallowed. However this did not stop him wanting to lecture him for the last time with all the authority conferred on him by the deathbed.

'This time you must listen to me,' he told him, 'for I am about to go.'

'I listened to you throughout my childhood and throughout my youth,' Gilles replied, 'I'm not sure that your counsel has always been good for me.'

36

'Don't be ungrateful. I have worked long and hard to amass my own fortune, that's true.'

'. . . long and hard – violently, perfidiously and unscrupulously,' Gilles added.

'. . . my own fortune,' Craon continued, unperturbed. 'But as you are my sole heir, this fortune is also yours. You are very rich, my grandson. After my death you will be immensely rich. You will be master of Blaison, Chemillé, La Mothe-Achard, Ambrières, Saint-Aubin-de-Fosse-Louvain, seigneuries that come from your father. From your mother, you will have those of Briollay, Champtocé, Ingrandes, La Bénate, Le Loroux-Botereau, Sénéché, Bourgneuf and La Voulte. Then, thanks to the marriage that I made for you with the Thouars heiress, you have Tiffauges, Pouzauges, Chabanais, Gonfolenc, Savenay, Lambert, Gretz-sur-Maine and Châteaumorant. Truly, my grandson, you are one of the wealthiest lords of your time.'

Gilles had not been listening to this tedious enumeration.

'You know very well these things mean nothing to me,' he said.

'You know how to spend better than anybody. But that's how it is. The grandsons squander what the grandfathers have built up.'

'You seem to forget,' Gilles replied, 'that I have had another master than you, another mistress, I don't know quite how to put it.'

On the contrary, Craon knew perfectly well how

to put it.

'That boy-girl, known as the Maid, who was condemned by the church and burnt last year at Rouen? You always did keep deplorable company!'

Gilles preferred the litanies of the Janus-Jeanne to his grandfather's enumerations of all his worldly goods.

'Jeanne the holy, Jeanne the chaste, Jeanne the victorious under the standard of St Michael! Jeanne the monster in woman's shape, condemned to the stake for sorcery, heresy, schismaticism, change of sex, blasphemy and apostasy,' he recited.

'So there you are, hanging strangely between heaven and hell. I confess I would rather have had for my heir an old, rough soldier who drank himself stupid, raped women, and was as intelligent as a donkey!'

'I swore to follow her wherever she went, to heaven or to hell.'

'And she ended up on the witches' stake! You frighten me, my grandson. May God preserve you from excessive sanctity. At least all I can be reproached with is having built up my fortune without too much scruple and I have never killed any man unless self-interest absolutely required it. I fear those who kill for disinterested motives! Why should they ever stop? Greed kills a thousand times fewer men than fanaticism. So my greed will place an immense fortune at the service of your fanaticism. I tremble to think what will come of it all!'

The villeins of the seigneury of Machecoul-en-Rais were the first to know the answer to that question. There Gilles founded a community dedicated to the Holy Innocents. Nothing seemed to him too fine or too dear to honour those young boys killed on King Herod's orders. Eighty men – a dean, cantors, archdeacons, vicars, scholars, treasurers, coadjutors – maintained in splendour, devoted themselves to their memory. The ornaments and treasury of the community rivalled those of a cathedral. The ceremonies and processions through the countryside displayed a pomp that dumbfounded those who saw them pass. The gold, the purple, the minever, the silk, the lace, the brocade formed a background worthy of the monstrances, ciboria, candlesticks and croziers held aloft. The canons wore capa magna, the cantors wore mitres, the very horses advanced with censers swinging from their necks and caparisoned like prelates.

But it was by the choir that the master set greatest store. Out of personal inclination and because nothing was fitter than a choir of angelic boys to honour the innocents slaughtered at Bethlehem, Gilles was tireless in recruiting and examining the young singers of his foundation from the point of view of their voices – and the rest. Indeed it was not enough that they should have a divine voice, since, being divine, they should also look divine in face and body. As for the music that they were taught, Gilles expected only one thing: that it should break his heart. Was not that the least one might expect of an institution intended to celebrate the great massacres of the boys born in the same year as Jesus?

But that was not all. A renowned artist was commissioned to cover the chapel walls with a vast fresco depicting that bloody episode in St Matthew's gospel. The artist had spared no detail and his vision was all the more striking in that, according to the practice of the time, he had costumed his figures like the men, women, and children of his own period, and placed them in a village that was supposed to be Bethlehem, but in which everybody could recognize the houses of Machecoul. So the villeins who ventured into the chapel might well think that they recognized themselves on its walls, and not only themselves, but also the soldiers of the castle and even their lord Rais behind the features of the cruel

King of the Jews. And the anguished chants of the angel-faced choirboys moved Gilles all the more intensely when he saw those children against the background of such horror and slaughter. Overcome with emotion, he would stand there leaning against a pillar, murmuring between sobs, 'Pity, pity, pity!'

And this compassion that he felt became so ardent that he began to feel scruples about it and, one day, he opened his heart to his confessor, Father Eustache Blanchet.

'Father, is pity a Christian feeling?' he asked.

Blanchet was an uncomplicated soul and sincerely believed that there was a simple, obvious answer to all questions of faith and morals.

'Certainly, certainly, my son, for is not pity the sister of mercy and therefore the cousin of charity?'

Gilles wiped away his tears and reflected for a moment.

'The sister of mercy and the cousin of charity perhaps, but, all the same, it is a quite different feeling. What disturbs me in the pity I feel is . . .'

Blanchet came to the assistance of his spiritual son, who seemed to be on the verge of making some confession that was difficult to put into words.

'Do not hesitate, my child, open your great heart to your confessor, as to your Holy Mother the Church.'

'What disturbs me, yes, what disturbs me in pity is the immense pleasure I find in it.'

Blanchet felt at once that he was beginning to get

41

out of his depth.

'Immense pleasure? Explain, my son!'

'I have pity on those boys that are slaughtered, I weep over their tender, panting bodies, and yet I feel such pleasure in it! It is so moving to see a child suffering! A tiny bloodstained body in its death throes is such a beautiful sight!'

Blanchet really was at a loss how to reply. Gilles then gripped him by the arm, leaned towards him as if to whisper some secret into his ear and asked: 'Father, is such pity from God or from the Devil?'

The condition of the confessor is ambiguous, sometimes dizzily so! He is only God's medium before the penitent. The ear with which he listens to the penitent's avowals and revelations is not human. And the duty of absolute secrecy by which he is bound – and no pressure or persuasion, no threats or promises, no tortures can break it – derives from that equivocal situation. As soon as he is outside the confessional, as soon as he has taken off his stole, the confessor becomes once more a poor man like other men. Not only can he not divulge what he has just heard, but has he even the right to remember it in his dealings with his penitents, once they have become once more ordinary companions, subordinates and masters? And yet, and yet . . . His earthly ear had heard and remembered!

Gilles had made avowals to Eustache Blanchet

43

that, taken together with certain rumours that had been heard and certain scenes that had been glimpsed, might have enabled the confessor to see more clearly. But Blanchet refused to mix what he had heard in confession with what profane life brought him on its impure tide. And anyway the truth that he sensed prowling around him was so terrible, it would have required of him such far-reaching decisions that he preferred as long as possible – but for how many days more could it last? – to retreat timidly to his daily tasks as chaplain.

It all started with these boys that had to be recruited and examined for entry to the choir school. Gradually Gilles had taken such pleasure in this sort of prospecting that he pursued it well beyond the needs of the community, beyond all reasonable measure, even to the extent of abandoning the pleasure of hunting – which had formerly played such an important role in his life – in order to chase that other game, which was so special and so delicious. And as he was such a powerful man, with such large forces at his disposal, he soon gathered together a handful of beaters and strong-arm men who scoured the woods and countryside. Fantastic stories spread regarding their activities. Dark, cruel scenes were inscribed with all the power of legend in popular imagery.

There was shown, for example, against a stormy sky, the dark outline of a horseman galloping through plains and forests. He passes through a hamlet: the inhabitants flee and lock themselves in their houses. A woman rushes out after a young boy, seizes him and takes him into her house. The horseman is swathed in a large cloak, which floats around the horse. With loud beating of hooves he crosses the castle drawbridge. He is now standing, motionless, legs apart, at the entrance to the armoury. The lord's voice is heard.

'Well?'

The horseman opens his cloak. A young boy is clinging to him. He falls down, then tries to rise clumsily.

'Well done!' says the voice.

Or another picture comes to mind. The lord and his retinue are slowly riding through some wretched hamlet. Dumbfounded peasants watch them pass. They are thrown a handful of coins, which they fight over. Some of the inhabitants come up and kiss Gilles's hand or foot. The troop passes by a group of children playing in the dust. Gilles watches them passionately, holding his horse's bridle. He makes a sign to his servant Poitou. With the tip of his whip he indicates one of the boys.

'That one!'

Poitou goes towards the wrong one.

'The fair-haired one holding the ball?'

Gilles is getting impatient.

'No, no, you fool, the red-haired one who is doing nothing!'

Next day, a horseman is seen giving money to

45

some artisans. The young red-head is there with his bundle of clothes, happy at the thought of going away. The boy is helped up on to the horse. They gallop off. The weeping mother makes the sign of the cross. The father counts over the money again.

There was also talk of a kind of witch. She was called Perrine Martin. But she was nicknamed La Meffraye (she who arouses fear). Passing through a village, she attracted the attention of a young boy, luring him like a young animal with a piece of cake or bacon to some deserted place. There men in ambush threw themselves upon him, bound and gagged him, and carried him off in a sack.

Then there was the case of the boy who resisted and had a good pair of legs. His parents had sold him to Gilles's men, but he ran away from home. They looked for him in vain. Gilles, bitterly disappointed, dashed off in pursuit, with a pack of hounds. What exhilaration he felt recapturing those former pleasures, but this time hunting a human prey! Indeed it was a classic chase, with breaking cover, beating, getting ahead, and finally the pack baying at the foot of a beech tree, with the little boy perched in its branches.

The most terrible of these stories that were passed on in hushed tones was later to become part of the treasury of French fairy tales.

It begins in the wretched hovel of a woodcutter and his family. This tiny space swarms with seven children, three pairs of twins and a last child, who is so puny that he is called Poucet, or Tom Thumb in the English version of the tale. The parents have the bestial faces that poverty gives to those who are not saints. The wife's filthy apron fails to hide her swelling belly. The husband pats her belly and says with a snigger: 'As long as I've known you, you've always been making us another pair of brats!'

The woman shakes him off.

'So with these here we'll have some more. And anyway you talk as if you have nothing to do with it.'

He laughs a self-satisfied male laugh.

'With you, I only have to touch you and, hey presto!, that's another two.'

'Yes, and we then have to see how we are going to feed them,' the woman reminds him.

'They're grown-up now, they can look after themselves.'

'Poucet is only just six.'

'Then the good God that sent them to us can look after them – or if he doesn't want to, then he can come and take them back!'

'Leave the good God out of it, will you!'

Soon afterwards the whole family goes off to the woods. Animals, large and small, stand stock-still, on the alert, observing them through the copses and foliage. They wind their way through the woods to a small clearing, where, growling in the forest people's dialect, the father hands round small baskets, plus a few clouts for those who complain of tiredness. They then disperse to pick mushrooms and bilberries. When the last of them has disappeared, the man makes a sign to the mother, who responds with a gesture of protest. He takes her forcefully by the arms and leads her off. Later, the children meet up again in the clearing. They are exhausted and hungry. They are surrounded on all sides by terrifying animal cries – owls, foxes and wolves. They form a pitiful group at the foot of a huge tree. The bravest of them is Poucet. He looks around to find a way out.

'I'm going to climb up the tree,' he says at last. 'Help me. From up there I might see a light.'

His brothers help him to climb up. Soon he has a view over the darkening forest, which rolls on to infinity. Yet very far, on the horizon, he can just see the dark, massive outline of a fortress. There is a light in one of the windows. It is the Château de Tiffauges. Poucet scrambles down among his brothers.

'We are saved,' he announces, 'over there there's a big castle that's lit up. Let's go there!'

The group plunges into the forest led by Poucet. Soon they arrive at the castle entrance. They knock on a postern. The gate opens as if by magic. They go in one by one. The gate shuts behind them.

Some time later, Blanchet was disturbed in his priory by a smell of burning flesh that infested the atmosphere. He went out and saw that a torrent of black smoke was gushing out of the castle's biggest chimney and was being blown back over the out-buildings by an east wind, which was fairly rare in that region. This stink of burning flesh consorted so well with his fears that he decided to seek out Gilles and without further delay demand an explanation. For a long time he looked for him in the innumerable halls and chambers of the castle. Eventually he found him up on a small terrace quite close to the incriminating chimney. Gilles was standing there and, in his terrifying exaltation, he resembled a man possessed by some dark obsession.

As soon as he saw Blanchet, he rushed up to him and laid his hands on his shoulders.

'Father, father, that smell? What is that smell?' he asked him, shaking him. 'Doesn't it remind you of something? Ah, you weren't at Rouen, were you? But, tell me, is it a savour of heresy or an odour of sanctity?'

Then he shut his eyes and started repeating in a voice that changed more and more, finally breaking into a sob: 'Jesus! Jesus! Jesus! Jesus!'

Next day Blanchet took to the road with three mules led by a servant. With some relief he had accepted a mission that Gilles had given him after a particularly delirious night. Word had reached the farthest reaches of the Vendée of the marvels that were taking place far away to the south, in Tuscany. Scientists, artists and philosophers, it seemed, had combined their forces and intelligence to create a new golden age that would soon spread to the whole of mankind. So he was to go and investigate these novelties on the spot! Perhaps he would bring back to the Vendée some teaching, some object, even perhaps some man capable of tearing the Seigneur de Rais from his dark chimeras?

The former little seminarist from Saint-Malo was dazzled and scandalized by the spectacle of that mid-quattrocento Tuscany. He had, of course, known wealth. The Sire de Rais, whom he had served as chaplain for four years, was one of the richest lords in the kingdom of France. But the Vendée displayed a poverty that was all the starker in that its lord was obviously squeezing it quite shamelessly to pay for his infernal way of life. Florence could not have looked more different in the year 1439. There the crowd seemed rich, even the ordinary people seemed to juggle with florins. Gold circulated in every street. What astonished Blanchet above all were the craftsmen, who seemed to work only for luxury and beauty. He looked in vain for ordinary clothes, finding only tailors ready to sell him princely garments. The smiths worked with neither iron nor

51

steel, but apparently only with silver and gold. The carpenters were all employed erecting palace cupolas. Even the bakers displayed no bread on their stalls, only cakes made with cream and honey. Could it be, then, that these people – even the lowest of the low – were all rich?

His strange appearance and obvious trepidation attracted the attention of an undesirable assortment of rogues and vagabonds, awaiting a good opportunity to strip him bare. Such an opportunity arose when Blanchet, who did not yet know the city, strayed into a blind alley. Finding that he could go no further, he turned round to retrace his steps. Three evil-looking individuals barred his way and upbraided him in some indecipherable dialect. Blanchet imagined that they were vehemently reproaching him for entering that place. He began to apologize in his own language, but the three villains surrounded him, moved in upon him and began to search him. Blanchet was at a loss to know which saint to invoke. If he called for help, would not these thieves do what was required to silence him? So he was standing there, transfixed with fear, when an order, uttered in a commanding voice, was heard and the three pairs of filthy hands, which a moment before had been weaving in and out of his clothes, suddenly vanished like a cloud of magpies. A most elegantly attired stranger, attended by two armed servants, was standing, legs apart and arms crossed, at the entrance to the alley. After a few more words in low Tuscan, the thieves disappeared into the night. The stranger approached.

'Thank you, my lord,' Blanchet stammered, 'you have saved my life. I am the Abbé Eustache Blanchet.'

'You're French,' the stranger observed. 'I am Francesco Prelati. You can call me François Prélat if it makes it any easier. The blackguards who were importuning you are small fry – too small to kill. They only wanted your money – unless your clerical dress led them to believe you might have some relics about your person. Nobody is more enamoured of relics than such petty thieves. Have you supped?' he went on, without transition. 'If not, I cordially invite you to eat with me – with the money I had the good fortune to save for you.'

And without waiting for an answer, he led Blanchet off. The Frenchman was still amazed by everything that had happened to him. Since his saviour never paused for a moment to draw breath, the abbé very soon knew a great deal about him. He was twenty years old and a native of Monte Catini, in the diocese of Lucca. He was a clerk and had received the tonsure from the Bishop of Arezzo. In Florence, he had studied poetry, geomancy and alchemy. For the time being he belonged to the house of the Bishop of Mondovi, knew Florence like the back of his hand and was a past master in the art of taming the undesirable creatures who roamed its poorer quarters – as he had just proved to the abbé. A few

53

minutes later they were in a trattoria, eating a good supper out of Blanchet's rescued savings, as the young clerk had unceremoniously decided. When the young man had paid for the meal, he lovingly stroked the priest's purse and said with a great laugh: 'You mustn't risk losing it again in the alleyways of this town. We've better uses for it!'

Blanchet concluded that he had been left without a farthing and was surprised that so well-attired a young man, attended by two servants, should seem so short of funds.

They parted, agreeing to meet up again the next day. Over the next few days they saw quite a lot of one another. Prelati had taken it upon himself to act as guide and protector of the innocent Frenchman, who gradually fell completely into his hands. Prelati showed him the splendours and mysteries of that city, which at the time was a vast building site for palaces and churches, with architects, painters and sculptors rushing hither and thither.

The Medici era had just begun with Cosimo's triumphal return from exile in Venice. But what were the Medicis? Above all they were men of money, bankers, specialists in various kinds of trafficking, lending on interest, and bills of exchange. Under their impetus Tuscany was to enjoy a period of unprecedented prosperity. Blanchet even had the good fortune to attend ceremonies whose splendour dazzled the whole of Europe. On 6 July, under Cosimo's chairmanship, there met an ecumenical

54

council in which the Pope, Eugenius IV, the Roman Emperor of the East, John VIII Paleologus, and Joseph, Patriarch of Constantinople, took part. These three spiritual and temporal princes, laden with gold, frankincense and myrrh, formed a procession through the city streets leading to the Duomo, a spectacle of such incomparable brilliance that it reminded the people of the cavalcade of the three magi on their way to Bethlehem. The Florentines' special veneration for the three magi, as illustrated in the works of Benozzo Gozzoli and Fra Angelico, dates from that time.

'And what is the meaning of the episode of the three magi in St Matthew's gospel?' Prelati asked, and proceeded to answer his own question. 'Notice how, unlike the shepherds, who placed milk, bread and wool – modest, but useful gifts – before the crib, the three kings, with their gold, frankincense and myrrh, offered the Infant-God gifts that were certainly of greater value, but quite useless, gifts of the most gratuitous luxury.'

When Blanchet dared to make a gesture of protest, Prelati hastened to add: 'Indeed Jesus took good care to remember the value of that superfluous splendour. Remember how, in the house of Simon the Leper, Mary Magdalene anointed his head with a perfume of great price. The apostles were scandalized by this prodigality, but Jesus took them to task. Was such homage too costly for the Son of God?'

And carried away by the logic of this teaching,

Prelati continued enthusiastically: 'Have gold, more gold and yet more gold and the rest will be given unto you, genius and talent, beauty and nobility, glory and pleasure, and even, by some incredible paradox, disinterest, generosity, charity!'

'Hold on, hold on!' Blanchet spluttered.

'And science, too, my good father, science, which opens all doors, all coffers, all safes . . .'

'I am dazzled by everything I see, but why, on top of everything, do you insist on deafening my ears with your extravagant words? Poverty is not a vice, for heaven's sake!'

'Poverty is the mother of all vices.'

'Prélat, my friend, now you are blaspheming!'

'If I locked you up in a cage with a lion, would you prefer the animal to be well fed or hungry?'

'It would be wiser, I think, that it were well fed,' Blanchet conceded.

'Well, men are like lions, like all the beasts, like all living creatures. Hunger makes them fierce. And what is poverty, if not generalized hunger?'

'And how do you see sacrifice, devotion, self-abnegation?'

'I give them the place that such virtues deserve – a minute one!'

'Minute?'

'Yes, minute. Take a thousand good, well-fed burghers, all inclined to benevolence to their fellow men. Shut them up in a cave without food and drink. Make them hungry! They will be transformed soon enough. If you're very fortunate, you may get one saint whose spirit will rise above the horrible condition of his body and who will sacrifice himself for his companions. One out of a thousand, with a bit of luck. As for the nine hundred and ninety-nine others . . .'

'Yes, what of the nine hundred and ninety-nine?'

'Those good, merry, benevolent burghers will soon become frightful villains, capable of anything, anything, I tell you, father, to satisfy their hunger and thirst!'

'To hear you talk, one would think that you had known such things.'

'In time of war, famine, and epidemics, do you imagine that such things are difficult to find?'

'And, above all, one would think that you took pleasure in such a frightful truth.'

'No, father, I do not take pleasure in it. But, you see, we Florentines have discovered a remedy for that purulent canker – gold. Against mankind's moral wounds, the panacea is wealth. If the good angel appeared on earth to cure all the wounds of body and soul, do you know what he would do? He would be an alchemical angel and manufacture gold!'

Was it because the population was incomparably denser in that province than in Brittany or the Vendée? It scemed to Blanchet that he had nowhere seen so many graveyards, charnel houses and gibbets. Tuscany was beautiful and the city of Florence opulent, but death lay in wait for you behind each tree, each street corner. Never had Blanchet encountered more repulsively sick or more cunningly mutilated criminals. Was one bound to conclude that this procession of dead or living carcasses necessarily accompanied, as their shadow, the wondrous inventions that had sprung from the Tuscan revival?

Prelati expatiated elegantly on this theme.

'I am astonished, Father Blanchet, that so profound a truth should have awaited Tuscany to present itself to your mind. What did they teach the seminarists of Saint-Malo? Yes, death is the obverse of life and one cannot reject one without rejecting the other. You see, the philosophers, scholars and artists of Antiquity had one major failing – they turned away from death. They wanted to know only life. Greek statues are irreproachable from the anatomical point of view. Not a muscle is missing and every bone is in place. But the Greek sculptors were capable only of observing the living body. No one in Athens or Rome opened up a corpse to see what is inside, how it is made, how it works.'

'The Greeks carved mythological gods and goddesses, heroes and monsters,' Blanchet observed.

'Precisely! Because they are eternal the gods are not alive. They do not possess that moiety of shadow, that promise of death, which accompanies every man from birth and which gives him his depth. But you Christians! Jesus died on the cross. His body was placed in the tomb. Innumerable saints have perished in martyrdom. Then why that superstitious fear of the human corpse, when it lies at the very centre of your worship?'

'Jesus rose on the third day, the holy martyrs have been chosen for eternal life. So what do you expect to learn from those corpses that you attend with such passionate concern?' Blanchet asked.

'That they yield their secret, the secret of life. Our surgeons are now daring to open up bellies and rummage among the entrails. Charnel houses, torture chambers and gibbets have found a purpose at last. We must plunge, Father Blanchet, we must have the

59

courage to plunge into the darkness in order to bring back light.'

Blanchet gave a shudder and looked away.

'You frighten me. There is something diabolical about your audacity.'

The word did not appear to bother Prelati.

'Diabolical? Why not? The Devil, too, might have a purpose. You just reminded me that Jesus rose from the dead, but I would remind you that first he descended into hell and spent three days among the dead.'

'Man cannot measure his destiny by that of Christ!' Blanchet cried.

'And Jeanne? What did you do with Jeanne?'

'She died at the stake.'

'Perhaps to reappear among us, transfigured when the time is ripe,' Prelati muttered mysteriously.

There was a crowd in the courtyard of the Medici palace when Prelati and Blanchet entered it at last. The latest work of Donatello, the most famous sculptor of the time, had just been installed there and art lovers, the pupils at the academies and a large number of the merely curious stood around. It was a bronze of David, the boy David, whose fragility and weakness had just miraculously vanquished the Philistine giant Goliath. Prelati had walked slowly round the statue and was now observing Blanchet, who was puffing out his cheeks and shrugging his shoulders.

'So that's modern art?' he grumbled. 'No, really, I can't see what . . . what . . . no really . . .'

'Don't you see that somewhat precious grace?' Prelati asked, with an intensity in which admiration for the work of art and irritation with his philistine companion were mixed. 'Don't you see that deliciously mannered, provocative attitude, that swing of the hips, which is justified by the fact that the left foot is placed on Goliath's enormous head? And those two spindly arms, like the delicate handles of a vase, the right hand holding the sword, the left a stone? And that odd get-up, that helmet crowned with bay and those greaves falling to the knees, with the rest of the body exposed? But that is not what is so modern about it, you see. What is modern here is the almost excessive presence of the anatomical reality of the body. The boy is looking down almost as if he were observing his own navel. At least his face, left in shadow by the edge of the helmet, helps to concentrate the spectators' attention on his navel. What is brought out in this statue, almost to the point of exhibitionism, is the chest, with its boyish, but well-defined pectoral muscles, the rounded neck-line of the thorax, the small belly, slightly swelling and thrust forward, the childish sex lodged between the tender thighs. Yes, there is a sort of smiling ostentation throughout that sensual, gay body. Never has flesh been so present in bronze.'

'It's extraordinary,' Blanchet murmured. 'You speak of this work both as a lover and as an anatomy

61

teacher. One wonders where the art lover comes in.'

'But that is precisely what the new art is about, my good Father!' Prelati cried, taking him by the arm and leading him out of the courtyard of the Medici palace. 'Yes, we have abolished the distance that artistic contemplation necessarily requires. So what is left? Love plus anatomy are left. We Tuscans are no longer painters or sculptors. We are lovers . . . for whom the skeleton exists. And not only the skeleton, but also the muscles, the viscera, the entrails, the glands.'

And turning to Blanchet, he yelled in his face with a terrifying laugh: 'And the blood, my good father, the blood!'

But while Prelati explained the Italian rebirth to Blanchet, Blanchet told his young friend of the dark, rainy forests of the Vendée and of the gloomy moods and sudden, unpredictable changes of his master, Gilles de Rais.

'The most exalting time of his life was that spent with Jeanne the Maid,' he related. 'For a whole year, they rode and fought side by side. It was they who freed Orléans, crushed the English at Patay and had King Charles crowned at Rheims. Then misfortune struck. Jeanne was wounded before Paris. Jeanne was taken prisoner before the raised drawbridge of Compiègne. Jeanne was condemned by the Church. Jeanne was burnt alive as a witch. Since that time, Gilles de Rais has abandoned himself with terrifying fury to every excess. He surrounds himself with extravagant luxury. He eats like a wolf. He drinks like a donkey. And,' he added in a low, almost imperceptible voice, 'he dirties himself like a pig. I would like to tear him away from that slough of despond in which he is wallowing . . . I am looking . . . I am looking for someone who can give him back a sense of direction . . . How can I put it? Give him back the vertical, transcendent dimension that he lost when he lost Jeanne.'

Prelati listened with passionate attention, realizing the role that he might play in that man's destiny.

'You say that everything went wrong for him when he lost Jeanne the Maid?' he asked.

'Yes, but in fact he lost her twice. At Compiègne on 23 May when she was taken prisoner and at Rouen, a year later, on 31 May, when she was burnt at the stake as a witch. Ah, that mad expedition to Rouen! I did all I could to dissuade him. He had no chance, no chance whatever of freeing Jeanne. When he came back he was not only downcast. It was worse. I could hardly recognize him. It was as if all the horror of Jeanne's death were imprinted on his face. He no longer had a human face.'

Prelati concealed beneath a relaxed air the fierce joy and curiosity that Blanchet's account inspired in him.

'No longer a human face, you say? That's really interesting! A face . . . what sort of face, then?'

'As I say, a bestial face. There was something wild about his features, almost the face of a werewolf. Yet, at the same time, it could be said that he had not really changed, he still had his old face.'

'Explain.'

'His flesh had not changed. He bore no trace of a wound or a mutilation. It couldn't even be said that he had aged. No, it was his soul. What disfigured his face was the reflection of his soul on his features. His face looked grief-stricken.'

'It was Jeanne's death that threw him into despair?'

'Despair? Yes, probably. Despair, but not sadness. Perhaps that is the worst thing about it. Gilles no longer hopes for anything. As I said, he has no way forward, no horizon, no ideal in his life. But don't think he moans and weeps! I wish he did! I wish he could! Alas, no, he laughs, he roars like a wild beast. He rushes forward, driven by his passions, like a furious bull. And he's strong, you know. Very strong . . . His strength . . . Some use must be found for his strength, it must be given some direction, raised upwards! Could you do that, François Prélat?'

He looked ardently at his companion, who responded with no more than an enigmatic smile.

In fact, poor Blanchet was struggling in the toils of contradictions that were torturing him. At every turn the spectacle of that new, but suspect civilization both enchanted and terrified him, just as Prelati's words brought to his mind inevitable conclusions that nevertheless he found unacceptable, being based on specious, but unassailable reasoning. And it was not just purely artistic innovations – like the use of perspective in drawing and painting – that filled him with wonder and fear. It seemed to him that the flat, edifying, worthy image of his pious childhood was suddenly exploding under the impetus of some magic force, was being undermined, distorted, thrown beyond its own limits, as if possessed by some evil spirit. When he stood in front of certain frescoes or pored over certain engravings, he thought he could see opening up in front of his eyes a vertiginous depth that was sucking him in, an imaginary abyss into which he felt a terrifying temptation to dive, headfirst. Prelati, on the other hand, swam like a fish in the new element produced by modern art, science and philosophy.

'First pierce the surface of things to see the ghosts moving about there,' he would say. 'Become oneself one of those ghosts . . . Through perspective, drawing flees towards the distant horizon, but it also advances and imprisons the spectator. You understand now, my good father? The gate opens upon the infinite, but you find yourself definitively compromised. That's what perspective is!'

Blanchet protested.

'Prélat, you frighten me! It's almost as if you took perverse pleasure in frightening me. And I wonder if I am not assuming a terrible responsibility in taking you back with me to Tiffauges . . .'

But tirelessly he came back time and time again to his master's unhappy state and the need to remedy it. And he could see no alternative but Prelati.

'Since Jeanne's death,' he went on, 'the marshal

seems to have been possessed by her ghost. I have heard him at night wandering through the ditches of the castle calling out her name. He seeks her face in every young person he meets. That desperate quest reached a climax at Orléans, on 8 May 1435. Six years before, the city had been delivered from the English by Jeanne. A great festival, ordered, organized and paid for by Gilles, was to commemorate that event. He commissioned a twenty-thousand line *Mystery of the Siege of Orléans* to be written and it was to be performed in sublime settings by five hundred actors. King Charles and the whole court went to attend the spectacle. Gilles squandered over a hundred thousand gold crowns on that festival. But don't imagine that this crazy undertaking was justified by a taste for luxury and a need of ostentation! Anyone who thought that did not know Gilles. No, it was not that, it was . . . something far worse.

Blanchet fell silent for a moment and, his eyes creased, seemed to be peering at his memory of the 'Mystery' to find the key.

'Yes, it was worse,' he went on, 'because it was the work of a mind made sick by his passion. Listen,' he said, taking Prelati by the arm and looking intensely in his eyes. 'That enormous, ruinous festival was, for Gilles, no more than a *lure*, in the sense in which huntsmen use the term. It was a sumptuous sacrifice to force – yes, to *force* – Jeanne's wandering soul to become re-embodied in the actor appointed to play her role.'

'Actor?' Prelati asked, surprised. 'You mean actress, I suppose?'

'No, I mean actor. For Gilles only bothered with youths. And, anyway, Jeanne was so much like a boy that it would have been more difficult for a girl to grasp her character than for a boy. So he recruited boys. They came flocking by the hundred, attracted as they were by the huge reward promised to the successful candidate. Each morning the same frightful comedy would be played out again. Gilles was approaching a climax of exaltation. He had probably convinced himself during the night that the miracle would take place the following day. He rushed about like a madman among the assembled youths, often shaggy-haired and half-starved, sometimes graceful of bearing and refined of feature. When a candidate was too far removed from the ideal desired – the bearded, maimed or simple-minded sometimes found their way into the crowd – Gilles would fly into a rage, beat him and kick him out. Sometimes he would pause, as if transfixed by a vision, take a boy by the shoulders, stare at him for minutes on end, but, almost invariably, he suddenly pushed him away, disappointed, with a cry bordering on a sigh and a sob. In the end, they had to come to a decision. Gilles went off, locked himself away and would have nothing to do with anybody or anything. The whole immense effort had been in vain. Jeanne had not come. She would not animate the prodigious festival given to summon up her presence. The steward himself chose an actor who would do the job competently enough. Gilles did not even give him so much as a glance.'

'And so Jeanne did not come,' Prelati repeated.

'Oh, yes, she came all right,' Blanchet continued vehemently. 'At least Gilles was convinced of it for a time. There was a young woman who claimed to be the Maid and to have escaped death at the stake. Note that Gilles had been at Rouen on 30 May 1431 and saw with his own eyes Jeanne's corpse, burnt to a cinder, tied to the post. But no matter! His desire to see Jeanne alive was so strong that he rejected the evidence of his own eyes. And indeed this woman so strongly resembled the Maid that she was recognized as such by Jeanne's own brothers and gifts were showered upon her by the burghers of Orléans.'

'Gilles did not care for facts,' Prelati remarked. 'He was seeking an adored face. He had found it. What else mattered?'

'You have never seen the Seigneur de Rais,' said Blanchet, with surprise, 'and yet, from what you have just said, you have already grasped the way his mind works. How will things be when you meet him for yourself!'

'I think I have understood the heart and soul of the Sire of Rais,' Prelati admitted. 'But go on. What happened to this second Jeanne?'

'She quite shamelessly married a lord of the Armoises. They had children. Nevertheless she was a good horsewoman and could handle a sword. Gilles was going to put a detachment of troops under her command and send them off to deliver Le Mans, as Jeanne was supposed to have delivered Orléans. But before doing so she had to get confirmation of her mission from King Charles. It was then that the whole enterprise collapsed. Cleverly questioned by Charles, she became confused and, in the end, admitted that she was an impostor. Yet another bitter disappointment for Gilles!'

T hus for hours on end they talked as they walked along the banks of the Arno, through the alleyways of the old city, on the ramparts overlooking the surrounding countryside scorched by the summer sun, and the two men – the little parish priest from Saint-Malo torn from the pious shadows of his faith and the defrocked clerk, the worshipper of the renascent sun – constantly came into conflict.

'Your arguments may have enslaved my intelligence,' Blanchet would say, 'but my feelings remain free and rebel against this rich, cruel Tuscany, this Florence so filled with marvels, yet so repulsive by its diseases. How I long to get back to the French countryside with its simple faith and harsh ways!'

Prelati replied to these protests with a loud, contemptuous laugh.

'Talk on, talk on, Father Blanchet, you know very

well that nothing will be the same for you as before your travels. You have seen too much, heard too much. Old Gothic man is dead, a new age is coming to birth within you. Whether you wanted to or not, you have eaten of the fruit of knowledge and you won't forget its taste in a hurry. And the proof: you struggle against my arguments, but you are taking me with you to see the Seigneur de Rais in the Vendée!'

'I am taking you because I can't do otherwise. Gilles de Rais has reached the verge of despair. He sent me to Tuscany in search of a saviour. I have found only you and I still hope that you will be able to help him. But you see how fearful I am. There is a great brightness in you, but I do not know whether it comes from the light of heaven or the flames of hell.'

This led Prelati off on to one of his favourite themes.

'The light of heaven and the flames of hell are closer than is often thought. Don't forget that Lucifer – the Bearer of Light – was originally the most beautiful of the angels. He has been made the Prince of Darkness, the absolute evil. That is a mistake! Man, steeped in mire, yet animated by the breath of God, needs an intercessor between God and himself. How do you expect him to enter directly into contact with God? He needs an intercessor, yes, and one who is his accomplice in all his evil thoughts and deeds, but one who also has entry to heaven. That is

72

why man feels the need to consult witches, to appeal to magi, to call up Beelzebub in magic circles.'

'So that is your modern science, nourished on blood and filth! You certainly give the devil his due! Not all science is good, Prelati!'

'Yes! All science is good! The only evil is ignorance!'

'There are secrets so majestic that their revelation would destroy the unfortunate man who allowed his curiosity to run away with him.'

'Knowledge gives power. If the mind has the strength to discover a truth, it also possesses the strength to master that truth.'

'There are powers that go beyond the capacities of a human being. Excessive power makes mad. What is a tyrant, if not a sovereign made mad by power.'

'Because that sovereign was an ignoramus. To each degree of power must correspond a certain degree of knowledge. What is to be feared, indeed, is unlimited power in the hands of a limited mind. There is no violence or crime that is not to be feared from strong hands in the service of a weak head.'

This image suddenly saddened Blanchet, who murmured almost to himself: 'Hands too strong, a head too weak . . . You have just drawn a very terrible portrait of my master Gilles de Rais. That master of twenty fortresses, that marshal of France has the heart of a little child. I see this very clearly when he lays that heart on my knee and begs me to forgive his crimes.'

73

Prelati shuddered at the last word.

'His crimes? The devil! Don't exaggerate, my good father!'

Blanchet felt that he had said too much.

'I was speaking of crimes . . . in the metaphorical sense. After all, you don't imagine that I was going to betray the secrets of the confessional!'

But Prelati was not a man to let such a fine, glittering word slip by.

'Who mentioned betraying the secrets of the confessional?' he asked gaily. 'Well, if there are crimes, we shall treat them with light! We shall see well enough what becomes of those swarming Gothic serpents when heated by the sunlight of Florence.'

They set off at last. Of the endless trek that brought them in a hundred days from Florence to the Vendée, Prelati remembered little but an immense, terrifying forest. The only trees that this city dweller had ever seen were in the scattered olive groves on the Tuscan hills. As he approached the Gaulish forest, he seemed to be plunging suddenly into a damp, vegetal element in which man had no place and the sense of oppression that seemed to envelop the two travellers as they entered that gloomy world was hardly relieved by the occasional sight of black-ened-faced, wild-eyed woodcutters. Indeed Blanchet did his best not to meet anyone as they crossed those lands infested with bandits and troops of errant soldiers.

At last the solid, gloomy mass of Tiffauges, which suddenly appeared against a wind-tossed sky, brought a human dimension to the endless sea of green. Prelati was soon to learn that the men among whom he was now to live were little more human than the forest that hemmed them in on every side.

The meeting took place in the castle banqueting hall. Blanchet, who had never seen Jeanne, could hardly have suspected that Prelati resembled her to a striking degree. At a distance, Gilles believed that what he saw was a hallucination. The Florentine walked towards him, as if illuminated by a light that gave him a surreal sharpness, while those around him seemed to merge into an indistinct background.

'Jeanne! Jeanne! Jeanne!' Gilles murmured ecstatically.

But when Prelati stopped a few steps away from him, the illusion could not but cease. Yet it left in him a lingering sense of wonder. The resemblance was truly an astonishing piece of good fortune – and how logical, natural, necessary it seemed!

'Welcome to Tiffauges, Francesco Prelati,' he declared. 'I have been waiting for someone for many a long year. I was beginning to despair. Perhaps you are the person I was waiting for. The future will decide soon enough.'

Prelati knelt to kiss Gilles's hand. Gilles raised him.

'So you have come from Florence and travelled six hundred leagues to see me. How did our Vendée strike you?'

'Tuscany seems to celebrate a perpetual spring,'

Prelati replied. 'The Vendée seems to be plunged into an eternal autumn.'

'Of course,' Gilles admitted, 'the south enjoys a pleasanter climate than our oceanic confines.'

'I don't mean the climate,' Prelati explained. 'The Florentine spring certainly means windows opening on to flowering bushes. But it also means eyes open on to sights that were once forbidden. Ears open on to truths as yet unspoken.'

'If you can give me such sights, such revelations and such truths, then I truly believe that you are the person I was waiting for.'

At this point Blanchet interposed and whispered a few words into Gilles's ear.

'My confessor is somewhat concerned,' said Gilles. 'He suggests that I ask you what such revelations will cost.'

'Whatever price they are worth,' Prelati replied unhesitatingly. 'An infinite price!'

Then Gilles and he burst out laughing and their gaiety increased at the sight of Blanchet's worried face.

Whether it was in honour of the newcomers, or because it was the eve of the feast of St Gilles, or simply a whim on the part of the master, that evening, at Tiffauges, there was a sort of ball. The music was in the hands of a band that was certainly impressive in size, but consisted entirely of bagpipes and serpents: it was, therefore, loud, but rustic and monotonous. The wines and meats continued to circulate and a great deal of both was consumed. As a result the company was bathed in a sort of jovial intoxication, fanned by the flames from the fire in the huge chimney, despite the mildness of the weather. Not the least strange thing about that ball was the absence of women. Prelati knew that the Seigneur de Rais's wife and daughter were living in retirement at Pouzauges. Nevertheless he was surprised by that crowd of guests abandoning themselves to those wild festivities, among whom there were very young boys, but not a single girl. He knew none of the dances – apparently they were folk dances – that sent the couples gyrating away from and back to one another, but he realized that most of them involved male and female roles, the latter being taken quite shamelessly by men – some of them not of the youngest – who seemed to be highly amused by this play-acting and had decked themselves out with ribbons, wigs and trains. He observed this court with fascination: how different it was from the one that he had left in Florence! It radiated a sense of brute force that both attracted and repelled him. Through the smoke, he saw powerful jaws, with several teeth missing, vociferating, laughing and devouring; hands covered with lace and jewels, but greasy and scarred, closing over viands or other hands; ardent, but witless eyes resting on him with cruel insistence. Were these creatures entirely men, or were they all more or less the products of matings with bears, wolves, or some other beasts of the forests of the Vendée? Foxes' eyes, wild boars' muzzles, badgers' beards, hairy chests hung about with golden chains and pectoral crosses, a hundred surprising details – flared nostrils, pointed ears that could be made to move, and the squeals, wails and hisses that replaced words and laughter as the night wore on – yes, everything about that ball suggested animal brutality and innocence. And not least the stench of wildfowl given off by that crowd suggested the closeness of ponds and fever swamps, swarming with life.

The sky was growing pale when Prelati wanted to retire to the apartment that had been put at his disposal. But he did not yet know his way about the vast castle and, after losing his way, found himself in a huge kitchen. It was a cruder version still of the banqueting hall. On the low tables were piled up quarters of meat, carcasses of veal, whole deer, pyramids of pigs' heads. A terrible matron, as round as a tower, with a Medusa face, busied herself among the cooking pots and spits, wielding a large kitchen knife. But what surprised Prelati most was the swarming mass of ragged, half-naked, filthy boys. However, despite their wretched appearance, they were muscular and apparently as happy as putti, as they elbowed one another and partook heartily of all that displayed butchery.

'How can I convert all that brute force to my subtle ends?' Prelati wondered, as he stretched himself for the first time on the monumental, four-poster bed in his chamber.

Autumn reddened the beech groves, blackened the ploughed fields and launched into the sky grey clouds that were constantly torn to tatters by the wind and rain. Gilles, escorted by a handful of men, roamed the country, accompanied by Prelati. Accustomed to the silence of sacristies, to the gloom of taverns and to the scents of ladies' chambers, the Florentine discovered the marshlands of Brière, the ocean shores and the island of Yeu. The sudden gales of the equinox took his breath away and he felt drunk with grandeur and desolation in that country where nothing smiled on the traveller. He learnt that God and the Devil whispered not only in the silence of the oratories, but that their mighty voices could also be heard in storms at sea. The time of secrecy, tears and sighs was now over, but with the tides of syzygy began the time of apocalyptic sound and fury.

On that day the horsemen were slowly picking their way across a landscape of dunes dotted with a few poor shoots of broom and gorse. They saw nothing but their horses' hooves disturbing mounds of dry sand, but the air was filled with the distant roar of the ocean. They fell silent, fearful of that invisible presence, stunned by the vast clamour of the waves, their lips salted by the wind-blown spray. Thus it must be when we approach the hour of our death and our familiar life seems unchanged as the beyond fills our ears with a deep chant that turns all our petty concerns to insignificance.

They arrived at last at the top of the last dune and discovered at their feet a shore where scraps of moss and seaweed galloped across the sand, pursued by the wind, and, further off, the furious ocean, white with foam. There was a moment of silent contemplation that froze Gilles's gloomy visage, Prelati's tormented features and Blanchet's fearful face. Each of them understood in his own way what the clamour of the ocean was saying. For Francesco Prelati, it was discovering the key to that desolate land that he had been seeking since his arrival. He recalled, like so many confused presentiments, his initial astonishment at the huge Gaulish forests, where the trees rose up like flames, peopled by a few blackened-faced charcoal burners, the hot, smoky castle kitchen and above all that huge ballroom chimney in which whole tree trunks burnt. For the Florentine the ocean represented the tool, the weapon that he now had in his hands, and at his feet he saw that vast liquid plain whipped up by the storm, that country of lagoons and swamps trampled with sea-spray, that downtrodden, humiliated people. Fire and water. To tear that province and its men from their horizontality, Florentine alchemy was sending them the most subtle of its fire-raisers . . .

He now knew the direction of his mission: to touch with an ardent hand the purulent wound of that country and to force it to rise, to stand up, as a prostrate cow suddenly gets to its feet on contact with a branding iron. Gilles was to be saved by fire!

So Blanchet was not entirely wrong in thinking that Prelati would influence his master in the direction of the sacred. That was certainly how the Tuscan adventurer conceived his role at the court of the Seigneur de Rais. But he was quite incapable of imagining the terrible course that this salvation would take. Gilles, stunned by Jeanne's execution, dragged himself along the ground like an animal. Prelati would raise him up, but only to encourage him in the diabolical vocation to which Gilles believed himself to have been called ever since Jeanne had been found guilty of the sixteen charges. The fact that Prelati had no intention of diverting his master from his criminal fate is shown by a little scene that took place one November evening in the township of Elven.

The two solitary horsemen, by the evident richness of their array, stood out against half-starved shadows that hugged the walls at the twilight hour. However, a villein barred their way and demanded to know their business. Prelati began to argue with him, but Gilles moved past him, attracted by the cries of children, laughter and whisperings. He directed his horse into a dark alleyway, stopped, undecided, and set off again, hearing once more the sound of children, followed by a stampede.

Meanwhile Prelati had managed to get free and set off in search of him. He, too, was guided by the cries of children. But soon he heard nothing more. In order not to be misled by the sound of his own horse's hooves, he dismounted and tied his animal to a railing. He thus came to a small square guarded over by a statue that was in such a sorry state that it would have been difficult to tell whether it was a Virgin or a Venus.

Gilles was there, surrounded by a group of ragged children, who observed him in deadly silence, the silence of birds hypnotized by a snake. Gilles was holding, close against his body, a boy of about seven or eight. The horseman's heavily gloved hand lingered over the boy's hair, then undid his clothes, closing at last around the delicate neck.

It was at this point that Prelati's voice rang out: 'Seigneur Gilles!'

Gilles looked like a sleepwalker who had just woken up. He stared around him wildly. He loosened his grip on the child, who immediately slipped away to join his companions. They all then fled, with cries that might have been either of triumph or of fear.

The two men faced one another for a moment. Then Prelati murmured: 'Yes, I know, I understand everything . . .'

Gilles's face became threatening. Then Prelati burst out laughing and, taking him familiarly by the arm, drew him away.

'I understand everything, I tell you. Bravo! Bravo, Seigneur Gilles! But not for nothing, I beg you! What I mean is, not just for the pleasure. At least . . . not only for that.'

They rejoined their horses, got back into the saddle and, as they moved off, Prelati's flow of words faded in the distance.

'That man who stopped us just now, do you know what he was? A priest . . . just a priest. A defrocked, excommunicated priest. Yes, the poor fellow was too fond of women, drink, gambling and money. But priest he is and priest he will remain for all eternity. The power given him to consecrate hosts or to forgive sins can never be taken from him. So he was offering us his services: invocation, possessions, black masses. That might be useful, don't you think?'

And as they rode away words pregnant with mystery echoed in the darkness: 'Death . . . sacrifice . . . there is a radiance beyond that . . . the power and the glory . . .'

From then on the Florentine used everything he could lay his hands on to convince his master that only a curtain of flame separated him from heaven and that the alchemical science alone would enable him to cross it.

'Fire,' he would say, 'is the worst tyrant, but the best of servants. One has only to know how to tame it.'

To tame it he set up an alchemical laboratory in one of the castle's huge attics. There was a forge, of course, with its hood, bellows and anvil, a foundry with its moulds and crucibles, but his main preoccupations were with the delicate arsenal of slow cooking: alembics, cucurbits, retorts, worms, pelicans and above all a majestic athanor, a furnace with reflectors, whose combustion was so steady that it resembled life itself.

86

The two men spent whole nights there, under the pink-granite roof, brushed by the silver beams of the moon and the wings of white ladies. Prelati always spoke under his breath and Gilles never knew whether he was talking to him, saying prayers or reciting magic formulas. The Florentine seemed to base his experiments on the fundamental ambiguity of fire, which is both life and death, purity and passion, sanctity and damnation. He maintained that the pilgrim of the sky – as the searching alchemist is called – never reaches one of those poles without immediately finding himself thrown towards the other pole by a phenomenon of inversion, as an excess of cold causes a burning, or as the paroxysm of love merges with hate. And this inversion could be either benign or malign. The sinner, plunged into the depths of hell, might re-emerge arrayed in innocence providing he had not lost his faith. The witches' stake was not a punishment, still less a means of ridding the human community of some accursed creature – like the profane death penalty. It was a purificatory trial intended, on the contrary, to save a seriously threatened soul. The Holy Inquisition tortured and burnt only in a spirit of maternal solicitude.

Hearing these words, Gilles was constantly reminded of the stake at Rouen where he had seen Jeanne twist and turn in the flames.

'She is saved!' Prelati declared. 'The saints had led her from Domrémy to Rheims cathedral where, beside the new King of France, she had undergone a sort of apotheosis. Then they had abandoned her and she fell from that profane pedestal. Her fall continued to accelerate to the bottom of the crucible of abjection: that stake and that charred carcass under the obscene eye of the populace. It was the zero level at which a benign transmutation was to begin. Washed by the fire of the sixteen charges laid upon her head, Jeanne had crossed the burning curtain that separated her from the celestial fields. From that point on her glory was certain to radiate. One day she would be rehabilitated and her judges, who had nevertheless been nothing more than the docile instrument of destiny, would be confounded. Later still, she would undergo beatification, perhaps even canonization[3]. But the trial by fire was the ineluctable pivot of this change of direction.'

Gilles now understood that if he wanted to follow Jeanne, he would have to continue the descent into hell that he had begun even before the Florentine's arrival.

'Barron awaits you,' Prelati whispered in his ear, 'Barron is calling you. Go to him, but not with empty hands. It is his carnal hunger that gives meaning to your sacrifice of all those children. Their flesh must open up to you the incandescent gates of hell.'

And he explained to Gilles that Barron's inveterate hunger for flesh came from far away, from on high. Do we not see how, in the first pages of the Bible,

Yahweh rejects the cereals offered to him by Cain, yet delights in Abel's lambs and kids? That meant, did it not, that God hates vegetables and loves meat?

And the Florentine burst out into demented laughter.

'Wretch!' Gilles scolded him. 'You blaspheme! And anyway what relation is there between that and the children?'

'What relation with the children?' Prelati exclaimed. 'The relation is that, in the end, Yahweh tired of all those young animals with which men stuffed him, then, one day, he turned to Abraham and said: "Take your little boy, Isaac, slit his throat and offer me his tender, white body!" Of course, at the last moment, an angel came and stayed Abraham's hand just as he was brandishing a knife over Isaac's throat. It didn't work that time, but it was only postponed. Jesus, ah that child, Yahweh did not miss that one! Flagellation, cross, spear. The heavenly father laughed with celestial pleasure.'

Such jokes hurt Gilles, who simply repeated: 'Wretch, you blaspheme, you blaspheme!'

Then Prelati would adopt an innocent air. After blaspheming, he would recite Holy Scripture.

'But you see, Seigneur Gilles,' he added, 'if Yahweh loves the fresh, tender flesh of children, the Devil, who is the image of God, shares the same tastes. How could it be otherwise?'

He came right up to him, took him familiarly by the arm and whispered in his ear: 'Perform the sacrifice of Isaac for Barron! Offer him the flesh of those children you have sacrificed. Then, instead of degrading yourself with them, you will save yourself and them with you. You will descend, like Jeanne, to the bottom of the burning pit and you will rise again, like her, into radiant light!'

What was then to take place, day after day, night after night, beneath the turrets of Tiffauges exceeds in horror what the most depraved imagination can conceive of. The master and servant – but who led that accursed game, who obeyed? – had abandoned the company of other men and, apart from two henchmen, Henriet and Poitou, who roamed the countryside and haunted the laboratory, no one knew what deeds were being wrought. Yet sinister rumours travelled across the country and, on St Nicholas's Day[4], a distinguished intruder penetrated their secret.

Gilles and Prelati were bent over the sublime labours of transmutation, when a soldier burst into the room. Prelati leapt at him to stop him seeing what was happening.

'Villain!' he cried, 'you are risking your neck! It is strictly forbidden to enter these premises, as you know very well!'

'My lord,' the man stammered, 'Father Blanchet sent me. A troop . . . a troop of many men, richly attired, are making their way to the castle. They will be here in less than an hour.'

'Good, good, now get out,' Prelati snapped, pushing him outside.

He seemed overwhelmed with grief as he looked round the room, chock-full with vessels containing liquids ready to get under way for the beyond. Then he grabbed an iron bar and began to smash retorts, jars and cucurbits. Gilles thought he had gone mad.

'What are you doing? Is it the end of the world?'

'In a sense, yes,' Prelati replied. 'Not a trace must remain.'

And he struck about him blindly. The mercury spread over the flagstones in puddles of silver. Books of spells curled up and blackened in the forge.

'Will you now explain what you are doing?'

Prelati stopped for a moment.

'Unfortunately, Seigneur Gilles, I know that troop of men advancing on Tiffauges. For a week now I have had its route observed by my men and I was hoping that they would spare us their visit. But no, in an hour they will be here. Nothing can stop them, the fine gentlemen of the court.'

'The gentlemen of the court?'

'The Dauphin Louis, the future Louis XI, if my calculation is correct. He's only sixteen, but he has the reputation of a sly mind in a weak body. He is already intriguing against his father King Charles.'

Indeed, the Dauphin Louis had taken up residence in the Château de Montaigu. The King had sent him into Poitou with the official mission of putting an end to the exactions of soldiers made sick by peace, but in fact to remove him from the court.

'That skinny cat is a bigot,' Prelati went on. 'He covers himself with medals and relics. His long nose recognizes only two smells: the odour of sanctity and the savour of heresy.'

Later the Dauphin was walking circumspectly through the halls of the castle, accompanied by Gilles and his retinue. He could smell something, it seemed, that was not entirely Catholic. He stopped before a chimney in which smoked shreds of parchment and bits of bone.

'What is that?' he asked, in surprise. 'Why were the chimneys pouring out smoke as we were approaching Tiffauges?'

Gilles tried to move him on, but he resisted and seemed absorbed in the contemplation of a fragment of retort.

'It is as if there were a smell of sulphur in these walls . . .'

'It is the vapour we use to expel vermin, my lord,' the Florentine hastened to explain.

'Vermin, truly?' said Louis, staring insolently at Gilles, Prelati and the men of the castle.

Then he resumed his slow, meticulous inspection, continuing as if to himself: 'There is indeed a great deal of vermin in the kingdom of France. But it is not of the kind that is exterminated with the vapours of sulphur. There is, it is true, a vermin of a particular kind that destroys itself by its own poisons. One has only to leave it alone.'

When the cortège had slowly formed again and

silently moved on, one could hear only the raucous cries of the jackdaws wheeling around the castle keep. But Gilles and his companions felt certain that some fatal threat now hung over them.

It has been said that Gilles de Rais's raid on Saint-Etienne-de-Mermorte weighed heavily in his arrest and trial. According to a simplistic, superficial logic, by which each effect has a cause and each cause an effect, this is no doubt so. But the process of destruction in that particular life was already well advanced.

The Château de Saint-Etienne-de-Mermorte had been bought from him by Geoffroy le Féron for practically nothing. Gilles had remained bitterly resentful of the fact. When he learnt that the new master was acting harshly towards peasants who were behindhand with their taxes, while he himself had not yet settled his debt, Gilles exploded in anger. On Sunday 15 May 1440, which was Whit Sunday, Gilles and his men rushed into the castle, pushing to one side an old porter who tried to stop them. No,

94

Geoffroy was not there. On the other hand, his brother Jean was celebrating mass in the church nearby. Gilles rushed into the nave, dragged the priest from the altar, threw him to the ground and threatened to strangle him. In the end, he bound him and took him off into captivity. This brutal attack lost him most of his remaining support. Following these events, Francesco Prelati delivered the following prayer:

'*Lord Barron, you are my witness that I have striven to the utmost to raise this man to your sublime threshold. I left my native Tuscany only to come and convert his violence to fervour and his base appetites to aspirations towards your august face. I believed that I had succeeded. And no doubt I had: was he not now sacrificing children, not out of base pleasure, but solely to offer you their remains as sacrifice? And what does he do then? Look how he has just done violence to a priest at the altar and dragged him off into captivity wearing all his vestments, without even stopping to think what he was going to do with him! And that over a matter involving a handful of crowns or a few villeins who had been hanged or tortured! Lord Barron, I confess that my disappointment is great and that I am strongly inclined to abandon the Sire de Rais to the deadly fate that he is forging with his own hands . . .*'

In fact, Gilles's isolation became worse over the next few weeks until he was finally abandoned at Machecoul on 14 September 1440, when armed troops from Nantes laid siege to the castle. The master looked dishevelled and drawn, crouching against the wall of one of the empty halls as the trumpets blared forth to announce the first summons, which was read by the notary Robin Guillaumet:

'We, Jean Labbé, master-at-arms, acting in the name of His Lordship Jean V, Duke of Brittany, and Robin Guillaumet, notary, acting in the name of His Lordship Jean de Malestroit, Bishop of Nantes, enjoin Gilles, Comte de Brienne, lord of Laval, Pouzauges, Tiffauges, Machecoul, Champtocé and other places, Marshal of France and Lieutenant-general of Brittany, to give us immediate access to his castle and to make himself a prisoner in our hands in order to answer before the religious and civil courts the triple charge of sorcery, sodomy and murder.'

Guillaumet's statement was received in silence, broken only by the cries of crows fighting over a carcass in the moat. Then the trumpets blared forth again to mark the second and third citations. At last Gilles got to his feet and, like a sleepwalker, began to roam the deserted galleries of the fortress yelling out the names of his companions: Prelati, Blanchet, Henriet, Poitou . . . Nobody answered. All had fled. Then, after more cries and tears, he came to himself. He dressed, armed himself and it was in the ceremonial uniform of a marshal of France that he appeared, after rolling back the great gate on its hinges. His appearance was so imposing that at first there was a misunderstanding. Jean de Malestroit's men, thinking that the Seigneur de Rais was attacking them at the head of a detachment of troops, fled in disorder. But no, to their astonishment, he was alone. Somewhat fearfully they surrounded him. He handed over his sword to the commanding officer of the troop. A horse was brought for him and he was respectfully helped to mount it. The cortège set off, but one would have been forgiven for thinking that they were his men and that he was still lord and master.

On his arrival in the courtyard of the ducal palace of Nantes, he was received by servants and taken to apartments in the New Tower that had been prepared for him. He doffed his uniform and put on the white habit of a Carmelite friar. He then knelt down at a prie-dieu and meditated, his head in his hands.

For Jean de Malestroit, Bishop of Nantes, chancellor of the Duke of Brittany and president of the tribunal that was about to meet, it was the prelude to the severest ordeal in his career. He reread the letter by which he himself had triggered off this shocking affair:

> *Let it be known that, visiting the parish of Sainte-Marie of Nantes, in which Gilles de Rais often resided, and visiting other parish churches, there came to our ears first the frequent public rumour, then the complaints and declarations of many good, discreet persons, according to which the Sire Gilles de Rais,*

97

knight, lord of the said place and baron, subject to our court, with certain of his accomplices, had cut the throats, killed and murdered in a most odious way several young innocent boys, after practising with these children unnatural lust and the vice of sodomy, often performed and caused to be performed the horrible calling-up of devils, sacrificed to these devils and made pacts with them, and perpetrated other heinous crimes within the limits of our jurisdiction . . .

The arrest and trial of Gilles de Rais in that autumn of 1440 set the whole city of Nantes abuzz. The ordinary people passionately discussed this affair of lords. Would the prisoner be put to judicial torture? The rabble hoped so, without really believing that he would be: the great ones of this world do not torture one another! Torture is good only for the people. No doubt the Marshal of France would emerge unscathed from the adventure and even more of a great lord than before.

For the minor adventurers of commerce and the law, the whole business was quite obviously a matter of money. Those half-baked tales of witchcraft and murdered children were just a smoke screen to conceal what was really at stake – that immense fortune, those fortresses, those lands, all that countless loot! It was high-flying banditry, with a regal quarry on which all the great wild beasts of the region were converging! Meanwhile, the sheer magnitude of the catch made Rais's enemies hesitate. A fable, improvised for the occasion, began to go the rounds: the rabbits had caught the wolf in the trap. What were they to do? What were they to do? After all, they could not set him free!

But, in high places, more noble concerns furrowed men's brows. Jean V, Duke of Brittany, and Bishop Jean de Malestroit bore the whole weight of this historic trial.

'What disturbs me, Monseigneur, is the ineluctable connection that will be made between this trial and that of Jeanne the Maid.'

'I see no connection between these two affairs,' Malestroit declared, without much conviction.

'But Gilles de Rais was Jeanne's faithful companion. And nine years ago Jeanne was burnt at the stake for witchcraft. And today what charge is being levelled at the Seigneur de Rais?'

'I don't believe I am sticking my neck out much if I say that he, too, is running a strong risk of ending up on the stake for witchcraft,' Malestroit admitted.

'You see!'

The two men lowered their heads in silence, as if overwhelmed by the obvious similarity. The Duke then resumed, hammering out his words: 'Jeanne's trial was a criminal undertaking of prejudice and imposture. I want the trial of Gilles de Rais to be an irreproachable work of justice and serenity. I am depending on you, Monseigneur!'

The trial opened on Thursday 13 October and ended on Wednesday 26 October. Thirteen days during which Gilles de Rais displayed himself under three aspects – or should we say three masks, or perhaps even three different souls inhabiting the same man?

First one saw the great lord, haughty, violent and relaxed. Then, in the space of a night, he was transformed into a desperate wretch, both bestial and puerile, clinging to all those whom he believed could bring him help and save him. Lastly, he seemed inhabited by the memory of Jeanne and went to the stake as a Christian, radiantly at peace with himself and his God.

From the first day, at the hearing of the forty-nine articles of the indictment, Gilles charged at the prosecutor, Jean de Blouyn, and Bishop Jean de Malestroit like an angry bull. To Malestroit's question, 'Have you anything to say regarding these charges?' he replied: 'I have nothing to say regarding these charges, because I have too much to say regarding the mouths that have pronounced them. Seigneur Malestroit, Bishop of Nantes, and you, brother Jean de Blouyn, and you, brother Guillaume Mérici, and you others sitting on the right and left of those eminent persons, like so many birds of ill omen on the same perch, I shall say this: I am as good a Christian as you and have as much right to divine justice as you and I declare, before God, that you are not judges. You are butchers! What is in question here is not my crime, nor even my person, but my fortune and it alone – my lands, my castles, my forests, my farms, my coffers and the gold that you suspect they contain. If I were poor, do you think that I would be here to answer charges of supposed murders and other heresies? No, if I were poor, I would now be as free as the air, because all of you here present care not a fig for crimes and heresies. What is at stake is something else – something much more serious than crimes and heresies. What is at stake is the immense loot that your quivering nostrils can scent. All of you have already stooped to sordid manoeuvres intended to bring about my ruin. Behind transparently false names, you have negotiated the buying of this or that parcel of my goods on fabulously profitable terms. No, you are not judges: you are debtors. I am not a defendant: I am a creditor. When I have gone, you will fight over my remains, as dogs after the death of the deer tear out its guts and entrails. Well, I say no! I reject your presence. I appeal to a higher authority. Get out! Leave this place!'

This furious attack coming from so prestigious a lord as Rais disconcerted the judges. A movement of hesitation ran through their ranks. In the end, one of them rose, soon imitated by the others. Downcast, they left shamefacedly, one after another . . .

The next hearing took place two days later, on Saturday 15 October. What occurred on that day is intelligible only if one bears in mind Gilles de Rais's unshakeable faith. No less than Jeanne – and like most men and women of that time – he lived on familiar terms with heaven and the Church was his mother. Indeed this is what he proclaimed at the beginning of the hearing:

'I am a Christian, do you hear, a Christian! Like you, I was baptized and therefore washed of original sin and put back in God's hands. And I might add that I confessed and received absolution from the lips of Father Eustache Blanchet the night before my arrest. As you see me now, your honours, I am as pure and white as a newborn lamb.'

But he was dealing with theologians more cunning and more ruthless than he. Jean de Blouyn then countered a subtle *distinguo* calculated to throw his ideas into confusion.

'You say, "I am a Christian." But one is not a Christian. Nobody can boast that he is a Christian, except Christ himself. At best one tries to become one. It is an inaccessible ideal.'

That was an example of cunning. The ruthlessness was to come from the lips of Jean de Malestroit:

'On the other hand, you do not claim to be a Catholic, and there, for once, you are not mistaken, Seigneur de Rais! For if you were ever a Catholic, you have ceased to be one, as you must know very well.'

'I have ceased to be a Catholic?'

'Exactly, you have ceased to be a Catholic – by virtue of a decree of excommunication taken in this very place, yesterday, concerning you, unanimously by all those present. You are excommunicated, ejected from the community into outer darkness.'

Excommunicated? The word struck Gilles like lightning. Excommunication was worse than death, since it led to eternal damnation. The soul cannot do without the protection of the Church in overcoming the traps laid by the Evil One.

Gilles emitted a howl of anger and pain.

'I? Excommunicated! You have no right! The Church is my mother. I appeal to my mother! I have a right to her presence, her assistance, her warmth. I am not an orphan. I am not an abandoned child. I have no wish to be left out in the cold far from my mother's bosom. Help! Help!'

And he dashed over towards his judges and threw himself, weeping, into Malestroit's arms.

The hearing was adjourned until the afternoon. Gilles, now in a calmer state, indeed transformed, made an act of submission to the tribunal:

'I recognize as competent judges of my case Bishop Jean de Malestroit, the prosecutor Jean de Blouyn and his assistant Guillaume Chapeillon, parish priest of Saint-Nicolas, and his assessors Guillaume de Malestroit, Bishop of Le Mans, Jean Prigent, Bishop of Saint-Brieuc, Denis Lohérie, Bishop of Saint-Lô and Jacques de Pontcoëdic, official of the church of Nantes. I humbly ask them pardon for the insults and wounding words that I addressed to them in my blindness.'

After this declaration, delivered in a low, monotonous voice, judges' caps, mitres, birettas and calottes nodded to one another: the gentlemen of the bench were consulting. Then Jean de Malestroit declared:

'For the love of God, your judges grant you the pardon that you beg.'

'Am I still excommunicated?' Gilles asked.

'The decree of excommunication is now lifted. You have been taken back into the bosom of our holy mother the Church.'

These words seemed to bring him back to life. He drew himself up and, looking down from his great height at the line of seated judges opposite, he said:

'For my part I recognize the absolute truth of the appalling evidence brought against me. There is not a detail of the testimonies made by word of mouth or by writing that is not correct. Since Christ died on the cross, burdened with all the sins of the world, no creature has had to answer for so many crimes. In truth I am the most execrable of men that ever was. The enormity of my sins is without parallel.'

There was so much pride in these admissions that the judges felt even more humiliated than they had done under the insults that Gilles had poured upon them two days before. Malestroit leaned over towards Blouyn:

'He thinks he's Satan!' he said.

'That is why,' Gilles continued, 'I beseech you to impose without weakness or delay the heaviest possible penalty, convinced as I am that it will still be too light for my infamy. But, at the same time, I beg you to pray ardently for me and, if your charity is capable of it, to love me as a mother loves the most wretched of her children.'

From this point on, Gilles stood, stiff and motionless as a statue, through the endless procession of witnesses, each of whom seemed, by his words, to throw another stone at his head. First came the parents of his victims, the children who had disappeared. There was Nicole, wife of Jean Hubert, of the parish of Saint-Vincent:

> '*I had a son named Jean, aged fourteen. He was approached at Nantes, where the Sire de Rais was staying, by a certain Spadine, who was living with the said Sire de Rais. This Spadine gave the child a loaf of bread, which he brought to us, saying that the Sire de Rais wanted him to stay with him. We agreed to this. Whereupon the child left with this Spadine and was never seen again. My man, Jean Hubert, went to the Château de la Suze to question Spadine*

as to what had happened to little Jean. The first time Spadine told him that he did not know. The second time, he refused to see Jean Hubert.'

There were other witnesses, like Jean Darel, of the parish of Saint-Séverin:

'A year or more ago, while I was sick in bed, Olivier, then aged between seven and eight, was playing with other children in the Rue du Marché, on St Peter's day. Olivier did not return home and nobody saw him again.'

Jean Férot and his wife:

'Two years ago on the feast of St John the Baptist, Régnaud Donète, now deceased, rented a place with us to practise the trade of baker, and often a son of his aged twelve would come and help him to put the bread into the oven. But several times we saw that, when he had prepared a half-oven full, if he knew that the Sire de Rais was in the town, he left the bakehouse and went off to the house of the said Sire de Rais. And we did not know what he did there. Now, one day, we cannot say exactly when it was, we saw him leave, and never, from that day, have we seen him again.'

André Barre, cobbler, living at Machecoul:

'Since Easter I have heard it said that the son of my friend Georges Le Barbier has been lost. He was seen for the last time picking apples behind the

Château de Machecoul. Some neighbours had said to Georges Le Barbier that he should take care of his child lest he be caught, for the rumour ran that at Machecoul they ate little children.'

Jeanne, widow of Aymery Edelin, dwelling at Machecoul:

> *'I had an eight-year-old boy who went to school and was very handsome. He was very white and very clever. He lived with his grandmother in front of the Château de Machecoul. He disappeared without me ever being able to find out what became of him. And about the same time, one of Roussin's children and another belonging to Jeudon also disappeared. And about two weeks later, one of Macé Sorin's sons was also lost. Since complaints were made, it was imagined that these children had been given, in order to free Messire Michel de Sillé, a prisoner of the English, who, it was said, demanded as ransom eighty male children.'*

Thomas Aisé and his wife, living at Machecoul:

> *'Being poor people, at Whitsuntide we had sent one of our sons aged ten to beg alms at the castle. We never saw him again or heard news of him: a neighbour's little girl, who had gone to the castle to beg at the same time, told how the girls had been given bread separately and that a servant had told the boys that they would have meat if they went into the hall. She saw them go in.'*

Péronne Lossart, living at La Roche-Bernard:

'*In the month of September, two years ago, the Sire de Rais, coming from Vannes, had lodged at the inn of Jean Colin situated opposite my house. One of the Sire de Rais's servants, a certain Poitou, took an interest in my son, who was then ten years old and was going to school. He asked me to let the child go with him. He would dress him and feed him very well and give him many advantages. I then told him that the child had plenty of time and that I would not take him from school. Upon which he told me that he himself would send him to school and give me four livres. So I let the boy go with him. And he took him to Colin's inn. Next day, as the Sire de Rais was leaving the inn, I went up to him and asked him to take good care of the child who was with him. He said nothing to me, but to Poitou he said that this child had been well chosen and that he was as beautiful as an angel. Shortly afterwards, they bought a young horse from Colin for the child and they set off. Since then, despite all my efforts, I have been unable to obtain news of my son.*'

T hey were soon to have news of all these children. The interrogation of Etienne Corrillaut, known as Poitou, and Henriet Griart, servants of the Sire de Rais, was to reveal what happened to them behind the walls of Tiffauges, Champtocé and Machecoul.

'After the Sire de Rais had transferred ownership of the Château de Champtocé to the lord Duke of Brittany,' Poitou recounted, 'he wanted to go back there for a last time with me. Before arriving at this Château de Champtocé, he stopped me and made me swear never to reveal what I was going to see.'

'And yet you are now going to tell us what you saw at Champtocé.'

'In the castle tower, there were children's bones.'

'Of how many children?'

'We had to put everything very quickly into coffers tied with ropes. I couldn't count them. But from the number of skulls, there must have been some thirty-six or forty-six.'

'And what did you do with those bones?'

'We transported them to Machecoul, to the Sire de Rais's chamber, and there, with his help, we burnt them in the fire. The ashes were dispersed in the castle moats.'

'What took place in the Sire de Rais's chamber at Machecoul?'

'It was there that Sillé, Henriet and myself brought the children that the Sire de Rais had been expecting.'

'Did you witness what the Sire de Rais subjected these children to?'

'Yes. The Sire de Rais, in order to take his carnal pleasure with these children, boys and girls, first took his member . . .'

'Silence! Not a word more!'

The prosecutor, Jean de Blouyn, rose to his feet, unhooked his cloak and placed it over the crucifix hanging on the wall behind him.

'And now, Poitou, continue!'

'. . . he took his member, rubbed it to make it stiff, then stuck it between the child's thighs, avoiding, in the case of the girls, the natural passage.'

'Could the cries of the children mistreated in this way have given the alarm?'

'To avoid those cries, the Sire de Rais suspended the child by the neck with ropes from a hook. Then, before the child died from strangulation, he untied

113

him, brought him back to life, tried to coax him, swearing that what he had done to him was not meant maliciously, but simply for amusement. Then, when the child began to be reassured once more, he slit his throat and again took pleasure with him during his agony.'

'How was the child killed?'

'Sometimes the Sire de Rais killed him with his own hands. Sometimes he got Henriet or me to kill him. The head was cut off or the throat slit open, or again the back of the neck was broken with a stick, in the way you kill rabbits. The Sire de Rais himself used a sword.'

On a sign from the prosecutor, an usher brought the sword in question and presented it to the judges.

With Henriet Griart, the court heard the finer details. First the prosecution wanted to know whether any of the children had survived their treatment at the hands of the Sire de Rais.

'It was not only as a precautionary measure, to silence them, that he killed them,' Henriet explained. 'More than once I have heard him boast that he took greater pleasure in killing and cutting the throats of boys and girls, watching them suffer and following the progress of their agony, than in taking his pleasure on them.'

'So not a single child survived the Sire de Rais's criminal embraces?'

'No, with one exception. When the Sire de Rais lacked fresh victims to practise his debauchery, he had recourse to the young singers in his choir. But then he was not so cruel with them, for he was passionately fond of music.'

'What did you do with the bodies and clothes afterwards?'

'The bodies were buried in the hearth under piles of firewood, and the fire was kept going until they were reduced to ashes and those ashes were then scattered over the castle's lands and waters. The clothes were burnt, too, but slowly, little by little, in order to avoid too much smoke, which might have aroused suspicion outside.'

'Were the children's corpses not previously used for various purposes?'

'Sometimes the eyes, the heart and the hands were laid on a dish. The blood filled a bowl. This was to make an offering to the Devil and thus gain his favours. But sometimes the Sire de Rais cut off the heads of several corpses and arranged them on the mantel. He then called us in and forced us to observe this display with him and to tell him which of the heads we found most beautiful. When we agreed on which one was the most beautiful, he took it in his hands and put his mouth on its mouth.'

The trial was to reach its climax with the interrogation of Francesco Prelati. The Florentine put into his appearance, his dress and his words all the insolent elegance that characterized him. This was not very astute, though he may well have considered that no calculation, no play-acting, no civility could save so compromised a cause as his[5]. Perhaps he was quite simply incapable of being anything other than himself. His haughtiness was evident in his first answer. The prosecutor Chapeillon asked him if he was called Francesco Prelati.

'Call me Prélat,' the defendant insisted.

'François Prélat,' Chapeillon resumed obediently, 'you were born twenty-three years ago at Monte Catini, in the diocese of Lucca, in Italy. You received the clerical tonsure from the Bishop of Arezzo, but nevertheless you turned to the study of poetry, geomancy, chiromancy, necromancy, and alchemy.'

That 'nevertheless' brought an ironic smile to Prelati's face, but was not denied.

'About two years ago, while you were lodging at the house of the Bishop of Mondovi, you met in the low quarters of Florence a certain Abbé Eustache Blanchet, who declared himself to be the confessor and envoy of the Sire de Rais. He asked you if you would be willing to help him in his work of salvation upon the same Sire de Rais. You accepted.'

'There was a soul in perdition, it was my duty to fly to his help,' Prelati declared nobly.

'So much solicitude on your part comes as a surprise, and it is even more surprising when one learns that in coming to the help of that soul in perdition, as you say, you called upon not God or his saints, but Satan, Barron, Belial, Beelzebub, in short, all the inhabitants of hell!'

'They alone could still do something for the Sire de Rais.'

'Explain.'

'Father Blanchet had warned me. Yet when I saw the state of abjection into which the Sire de Rais had fallen, I was frightened.'

'And you called upon the help of the Devil.'

'As far as God and his saints were concerned, Father Blanchet was there and he seemed to be at his wits' end. There is a proverb in my country that goes more or less like this: for a groom's illness, a horse's medicine. The medicine in this case was fire, above all the fire of Hell, which was alone capable of cauterizing the Sire de Rais's purulent wounds.'

'A strange medication that consisted in handing over Rais to the Devil!'

'It was not a question of handing over the Sire de Rais to the Devil. To invoke Barron, I composed the invocation of which this is the formula: "Come at my bidding and I shall give thee whatsoever thou wishest, except my soul and the shortening of my life."'

'Do you believe, then, that the Devil is to be treated in this way?'

'Certainly. You simply have to know how to speak to him.'

'And when you committed yourself to give him all that he wished, did you know what he wanted?'

'Certainly.'

'Human sacrifices! Blood, hearts, children's limbs!'

'Did not God demand of Abraham to sacrifice his young son Isaac?'

Malestroit could not bear any more. He rose in fury and, pointing at Prelati his mauve-gloved index finger, declared: 'Accursed Florentine, you outrage the Scriptures!'

Prelati turned to him, with ironic deference: 'And did not Jesus say:"*Let the little children come unto me*"?'

'I order you to keep silent!' Malestroit thundered.

'Satan is the image of God,' Prelati continued with

affected gentleness, 'an inverted, distorted image of course, but an image nevertheless. There is nothing in Satan that is not to be found in God. Indeed it was on this profound resemblance that I was depending to save the Sire de Rais.'

All these theologians, great lovers of subtle disputes, could not but cock their ears. Pierre de l'Hospital made a sign to Malestroit to allow Prelati to speak.

'Continue.'

'To drive the Sire de Rais to the blackest edge of wickedness, then, by the igneous operation, to subject him to a benign inversion, like the one that transmutes ignoble lead into gold. He was becoming a saint of light!'

'This is madness!' Malestroit cried.

'We are living in a time of madness. The Sire de Rais was thunderstruck by the tribulations of Jeanne the Maid.'

'What has Jeanne the Maid got to do with this affair?'

'The Sire de Rais placed his knightly heart in Jeanne's hands. She radiated sanctity. The angels watched over her. St Michael and St Catherine gave her counsel. After all she was going from success to success, from victory to victory. Then the malign inversion occurred: the dark night of prison, the trial, the condemnation, the expiatory, but also redemptive fire. The Sire de Rais had to submit, in turn, to that malign inversion. Hence his crimes under the invocation of the Devil. But he is now on the right path.'

'What do you call the right path?'

'Is he, too, not now on his way to the stake?'

'And what do you hope for then?'

'The benign inversion. Who knows whether, one day, the witch of Rouen will not be rehabilitated, washed of all accusation, honoured and celebrated? Who can say whether, one day, she will not be canonized in the court of Rome, the little shepherdess from Domrémy? St Jeanne! What light will then not fall upon Gilles de Rais, who always followed her like her shadow? And who can say whether, in this same movement, we shall not also venerate her faithful companion, St Gilles de Rais?'

On that Tuesday, 25 October 1440, one of those autumn storms that make one believe that the end of the world has come broke upon the ocean coasts. Huge waves battered the shores. Spray and foam were driven up into a sky ploughed with lightning and came to land in the narrow streets of Nantes. On the Ile de Biesse, one of the sandy tongues of land that obstruct the bed of the Loire, men struggled against the gusts of wind to erect a strange Golgotha: three stakes, surmounted by three gibbets, the one in the middle higher than the other two.

However the population was preparing for a splendid funereal festival. In the houses, the women and girls were dressing up as if for a wedding, except that they said not a word to one another and their clothes were black. For the festival that they would be celebrating that evening was the entry of the Sire de Rais into the other world through a door of fire.

Outside, the flames of a forest of torches twisted and turned in the wind. The great gates of the cathedral slowly opened. There first appeared, on the square, Bishop Jean de Malestroit, wearing a gold mitre and white gloves. He was supporting himself on his crook, as if weighed down by infinite tiredness. He had brought his heavy task to an end. But those thirteen days lay like twenty years upon his shoulders. Then came the canons of the chapter, in white albs and green cappae magnae, the ordinary clergy and the choirboys. They were followed by the Duke of Brittany at the head of his dignitaries.

In the procession a great void surrounded the three condemned men, Gilles, Poitou and Henriet, who walked barefoot and wore garments of homespun. Behind them walked the sombre crowd of the parents of the murdered children. They walked in couples, each carrying between them a small white coffin. They crossed the arms of the river by several bridges before assembling on the meadows of the Ile de Biesse. When he reached the foot of the stake, Gilles embraced Poitou and Henriet.

'I have asked and been granted my wish to die first,' he told them, 'lest you have any doubt as to my punishment. I shall precede you, therefore, to the gate of heaven. Follow me in my salvation, as you have followed me in my crimes.'

Then he turned to the crowd of parents and said: 'I testify that the faith of my childhood has remained

123

pure and unshakeable. I met a saint. I accompanied her in her glory. Then she was condemned by the Inquisition as a witch and I became the greatest sinner of all time and the worst man that ever lived. No one has greater need than I of the solicitude of his fellow creatures and the mercy of God. My friends, my brothers, I beg you, pray for me!'

The executioners busied themselves around the stakes. The flames leapt up. Three bodies swung in the wind. The crowd fell on its knees. Prayers and chants rose up. But neither this vast funereal choir, nor the deep rumble of the storm, drowned the celestial cry that echoed like a distant bell:

'Jeanne! Jeanne! Jeanne!'

Notes

1. (*page* 17) Isabeau of Bavaria, the unworthy mother of the Dauphin Charles.

2. (*page* 20) The kings of France, from Philippe Auguste in 1179 to Charles X in 1825, were consecrated in Rheims. There were three exceptions: Henri IV, consecrated at Chartres; Napoleon, consecrated in Paris, and Louis XVIII, who was not consecrated.

3. (*page* 88) Rehabilitated in 1456, Jeanne was beatified in 1909 and canonized in 1920.

4. (*page* 90) In December 1439.

5. (*page* 117) Condemned to imprisonment for life, Prelati escaped and joined the service of René of Anjou as a thaumaturgist. His employer appointed him captain of La Roche-sur-Yon, where he was joined by his colleague Eustache Blanchet. However, in 1445, he was tried and hanged for stealing and using the seal of the Treasurer of Brittany.